CW00621205

· GLOVEBOX ATLAS

FRANCE

AND BENELUX

1st edition March 1991

© The Automobile Association 1991

Published by The Automobile Association, Fanum House,
Basing View, Basingstoke, Hampshire RG21 2EA

ISBN 0 7495 0169 3

Produced by the Cartographic Department of
The Automobile Association.

Printed by Graficromo SA, Cordoba, Spain.

A CIP catalogue record for this book is available from the
British Library.

Contents

Driving in France and the Low Countries
IV

Journey planning map
X

Map pages
XII

Map symbols
1

Road atlas – Benelux
2

Road atlas – France
10

Index and city plans
45

Distance Chart
84

City plans included within index

Amsterdam • Antwerpen • Bordeaux • Brugge • Bruxelles • Den Haag • Lille • Luxembourg • Lyon • Marseille • Nice • Paris • Rotterdam • Strasbourg

Driving in France and the Low Countries

Introduction

Motoring laws in France and Benelux are just as wide-ranging and complicated as those in the UK, but they should cause little difficulty to the average British motorist. Regulations are given for each of the countries featured in this atlas. (Motoring regulations in Monaco are generally the same as in France. However, although caravans are permitted to pass through the principality, they are not permitted to stop or park.)

The AIT

The AIT is the international association of motoring clubs, to which the AA and its sister clubs are affiliated. Many offer reciprocal arrangements to members travelling abroad.

In **France** and **Monaco** the AA is affiliated to the Association Francaise des Automobilistes (AFA), 9 rue Anatole-de-la-Forge, F-75017 Paris. *Tel*: 42278200.

The Touring Club Royal de Belgique (TCB) in **Belgium** has its head office at 1040 Bruxelles, 44 rue de la Loi, Brussels. *Tel*: (02) 2332211. It is open weekdays 09.00-18.00 hours; Saturday 09.00-12.00 hours. There are branches in most towns. These are open weekdays 09.00-12.30 hrs (Mon from 09.30) and 14.00-18.00 hrs; Saturday 09.00-12.00 hrs. All offices are closed on Saturday afternoons and Sundays.

The Automobile Club du Grand-Duché de Luxembourg (ACL) has its head office at 13 route de Longwy, **Luxembourg**. *Tel*: 450045. Office hours are 08.30-12.00 hrs and 13.30-18.00 hrs from Monday to Friday; closed Saturdays and Sundays.

The Koninklijke Nederlandse Toeristenbond (ANWB) in the **Netherlands** has its headquarters at 2596 EC Den Haag, Wassenaarseweg 220. *Tel*: (070) 331131. The club has offices in most provincial towns. Offices are usually open between 08.45 and 16.45 hrs Monday to Friday and 08.45 and 12.00 hrs on Saturdays. Traffic information can also be obtained from the ANWB at the above telephone number.

Breakdowns

You are advised to seek local assistance as, at the present time, there is no road assistance service provided by a member club in **France**. The use of a warning triangle or hazard warning lights is compulsory in the

event of an accident or breakdown. It is recommended that a warning triangle is always carried. The triangle must be placed on the road 30 metres (33 yards) behind the vehicle and clearly visible from 100 metres (110 yards). Note — if your vehicle is equipped with hazard warning lights, it is also compulsory to use them if you are forced to drive temporarily at a greatly reduced speed.

The **Belgian** motoring club (TCB) maintains an efficient 24-hour breakdown service known as Touring Secours/Touring Wegenhulp. The Flemish Automobile Club (VAB-VTB), which operates in the Flemish area only, and the Royal Automobile Club of Belgium (RACB) have patrol cars displaying the signs 'Wacht op de Weg' or 'RACB', but as neither is affiliated to the AA, motorists would have to pay for their services. The use of a warning triangle is obligatory in the event of a breakdown or accident. The triangle must be placed 30 metres (33 yards) behind the vehicle on ordinary roads and 100 metres (110 yards) on motorways. It must be visible for a distance of 50 metres (55 yards).

The Automobile Club du Grand-Duché de **Luxembourg** (ACL) operates a 24-hour road assistance service throughout the whole country. The vehicles of the ACL are yellow with a black inscription 'Automobile Club Service Routier'. This service should not be confused with the 'Depannages Secours Automobiles' (DSA), which is a commercial enterprise and not connected with the AA or any other organisation. The use of a warning triangle is compulsory in the event of an accident or breakdown. The triangle must be placed on the road about 100 metres (110 yards) behind the vehicle to warn following traffic of any obstruction.

The ANWB maintains a 24-hour road patrol service (Wegenwacht) which operates throughout the **Netherlands**. In the event of a breakdown or an accident a motorist may use either a warning triangle or hazard warning lights. However, it is compulsory to carry a warning triangle outside built-up areas as hazard warning lights may be damaged or inoperative.

Accidents

France — Fire tel: 18. **Police** tel: 17. **Ambulance**, use the number given in the telephone box or, if not given, call the police (brigade de gendarmerie). If you are involved in an accident you must complete a constat a l'amiable before the vehicle is moved. This represents the European Accident Statement Form, and must be signed by the other party. In the event of a dispute and a refusal to complete the form, you should immediately obtain a constat d'huissier. This is a written report from a bailiff (huissier). A bailiff can usually be found in any large town and will charge a fee of Fr400 for preparing the report. The police are only called out to accidents when someone is injured, a driver is under the influence of alcohol, or if the accident impedes the traffic flow. When attending an accident the police prepare a report known as a proces verbal. The French authorities, at their discretion, may request a surety payment to cover the court costs or fines.

Belgium — Fire and **Ambulance** *tel*: 100. **Police** *tel*: 101. The police must be called if an unoccupied stationary vehicle is damaged, or if anyone is injured. If injury is involved the vehicle must not be moved.

Luxembourg — Fire *tel*: 012 — Civil Defence emergency services (*Secours d'urgence*). There are no firm rules to adopt following an accident. However, anyone requested to give assistance must do so.

Netherlands — Fire, Amsterdam *tel*: 212121. Den Haag *tel*. 3222333. Rotterdam *tel*: 4292929. **Police,** Amsterdam *tel*: 222222. Den Haag *tel*: 3222222. Rotterdam *tel*: 4141414. **Ambulance,** Amsterdam *tel*: 5555555. Den Haag *tel*: 3222111. Rotterdam *tel*: 4333300. If you have a serious or complicated accident, especially if anyone is injured, the police should be called before the vehicles are moved.

Emergency Messages

Emergency messages to tourists are broadcast by **France** Inter on 1829 metres long wave, Monday to Saturday from 25 June to 31 August. The messages are transmitted in English and German after the news at 09.00 hrs and 16.00 hrs.

In **Belgium**, emergency messages to tourists are broadcast daily on Belgian Radio in French and Dutch. *Radio Television Belge* (483 metres medium wave) broadcasts these in French during the news at 14.00 hrs, and after the news at 19.00 hrs Monday to Friday and 13.00 and 19.00 hrs on Saturdays and Sundays. *Belgische Radio en Televisie (BRT1)* (323.6 metres medium wave) broadcasts messages daily in Dutch after the news at 07.00, 08.00, 12.00, 17.00, 19.00 and 22.00 hrs. *Radio Television Belge (RTBF)* (16 and 49 metres short wave) broadcasts the messages daily in French at 12.45 hrs. *Belgische Radio en Televisie (BRT)* (50.89 metres short wave) broadcasts the messages in Dutch after the news at 09.00 hrs Monday to Friday, and on 198.4 metres medium wave between 19.00-22.00 hrs Monday to Saturday and 19.00 hrs on Sundays.

In **Luxembourg**, emergency messages to tourists are broadcast during the summer on the German *RTL* programme on 208 metres medium wave, and may be given at any time between 06.00 and 01.00 hrs.

Emergency messages to tourists in the **Netherlands** are broadcast daily on *Radio Hilversum* 1 in Dutch on 1008 Khz medium wave at 17.55 hrs. Between 1 June and 1 October these messages are repeated every day on the same wavelength at 23.02 hrs.

How to use the Phone

In **France**, insert the coin **after** lifting the receiver to obtain a continuous dialling tone. Local calls generally use a *Fr*1 coin or a *jeton* (special telephone coin bought from the point where the call is made), but two 50 *centimes* coins are sometimes required. Coins accepted are 50 *centimes* and *Fr*1, 5 or 10. International call boxes have metallic grey payphones. Cardphones can also be used for international calls. The charge for a call

to the UK is *Fr*0.5 for 11 seconds, with a surcharge if the call is made from an hotel. A reduced rate is available for calls made between 21.00 and 08.00 hrs.

Telephone codes — UK to France — 010 33
France to UK — 19 * 14
France to Republic of Ireland — 19 * 353
France to the USA — 19 * 1 (* wait for
second dialling tone).

In **Belgium**, insert the coin **after** lifting the receiver. The dialling tone is the same as in the UK. Use *BFr*5 coins for local calls and *BFr*10 or 20 coins for national and international calls. International call boxes are identified with European flags, and a call to the UK costs *BFr*25 per minute. Cardphones can also be used for international calls.

Telephone codes — UK to Belgium — 010 32
Belgium to UK — 00 * 44
Belgium to Republic of Ireland — 00 * 353
Belgium to the USA — 00 * 1 (* wait for
second dialling tone).

In **Luxembourg**, insert the coin **after** lifting the receiver; the dialling tone is the same as in the UK. Use *LFr*5 coins for local calls and *LFr*5 or 20 coins for national and international calls. International call boxes are situated along roadsides. A telephone call to the UK costs *LFr*75 for three minutes and *LFr*25 for each additional minute.

Telephone codes — UK to Luxembourg — 010 352
Luxembourg to UK — 00 44
Luxembourg to Republic of Ireland — 00 353
Luxembourg to the USA — 00 1.

To use the phone in the **Netherlands**, insert the coin **after** lifting the receiver. Use 25 *cent* coins or *Fls*1.00 coins (instructions appear in English in all public call boxes). When making calls to subscribers within the Netherlands, precede the number with the relevant area code. All payphones and cardphones can be used for international phone calls. The cost of a call to the UK is *Fls*0.95 for each minute. Local calls cost 25 *cents*. The cheap rate operates from 18.00-07.00 hrs on Saturday and Sunday; the charge is *Fls*0.70 per minute for calls to the UK.

Telephone codes — UK to the Netherlands — 010 31
Netherlands to UK — 09 * 44
Netherlands to Republic of Ireland — 09 * 353
Netherlands to the USA — 09 * 1 (* wait for
second dialling tone).

Motorway Tolls

With the exception of a few sections into or around large cities, all motorways (autoroutes) in **France** have a toll charged according to the distance travelled. On the majority of toll motorways, a travel ticket is issued on entry and the toll is paid on leaving the motorway. The ticket gives all the relevant information about the toll charges, including the toll category of your vehicle. On some motorways toll collection is automatic;

have the correct amount ready to throw into the collecting basket. If change is required, use the marked separate lane.

All motorways are toll-free in **Belgium** and **Luxembourg**.

Tolls are charged on some motorways in the **Netherlands.**

Speed Limits

In **France**, the beginning of a built-up area is indicated by a sign with the placename in blue letters on a light background; the end by the placename sign with a thin red line diagonally across it. Unless otherwise signposted, speed limits are:

Built-up area 60kph (37mph).

Outside built-up areas on normal roads 90kph (56mph); on dual-carriageways separated by a central reservation 110kph (68mph).

On motorways 130kph (80mph).

Unless otherwise signposted, the following speed limits apply in

Belgium:

Car/caravan/trailer

Built-up area 60kph (37mph)

Other roads 90kph (56mph)

Motorways and 4-lane roads 120kph (74mph).

In **Luxembourg**, the placename indicates the beginning and the end of a built-up area. Unless otherwise signposted, speed limits are as follows:

Built-up areas 60kph (37mph)

Main roads 90kph (56mph)

Motorways 120kph (74mph)

Lower limits apply to caravans. All lower signposted speed limits must be adhered to.

In the **Netherlands**, the placename indicates the beginning and the end of a built-up area. Unless otherwise signposted, speed limits are as follows:

Built-up areas 50kph (31mph)

Outside built-up areas 80kph (49mph)

Motorways 120kph (74mph).

Vehicles towing a single axle caravan or trailer are limited to 80kph (49mph).

Seat Belts

In **France, Belgium, Luxembourg** and the **Netherlands**, seat belts are compulsory, if fitted, for drivers and front-seat passengers.

Children

In **France** and **Luxembourg**, children under 10 are not permitted to travel in a vehicle as front-seat passengers if rear seating is available.

Children under 12 in **Belgium** are not permitted to travel in a vehicle as front-seat passengers except when using special seats or when rear seats are already occupied by children.

Children under 12 in the **Netherlands** are not permitted to travel in a vehicle as front-seat passengers, with the exception of children under 4 sitting in a special baby seat and children over 4 using a safety belt which does not cross the chest.

Currency

The unit of currency in **France** is the *franc (Fr)*, divided into 100 *centimes*. There are no restrictions on the importation of foreign or French currency, but amounts exceeding *Fr*50,000 should be declared on arrival. Travellers are restricted to taking *Fr*12,000 with them when leaving the country.

In **Belgium** the unit of currency is the *Belgian franc (BFr)*, divided into 100 *centimes*. There are no restrictions on the amount of Belgium or foreign currency that can be taken in or out of Belgium.

The unit of currency in **Luxembourg** is the *Luxembourg franc (LFr)*, divided into 100 *centimes*. There are no restrictions on the amount of foreign or local currency which you can take into or out of Luxembourg, but because of the limited market for Luxembourg notes in other countries, it is advisable to change them into Belgian or other foreign notes.

In the **Netherlands**, the unit of currency is the *Dutch gilder*, or *florin (Fls)*, divided into 100 *cents*. There are no restrictions on the amount of currency you may take into the Netherlands. Any currency taken in may be freely taken out, as may also any currency obtained in the Netherlands by exchange or by withdrawal from an account.

Documentation

A valid UK or Republic of Ireland driving licence is acceptable in **France** and **Monaco**. The minimum age at which a visitor may use a temporarily imported car is 18 years. In France a visitor may use a temporarily imported motorcycle of up to 80cc at 16 but must be at least 18 to use one over 80cc. (In Monaco up to 125cc at 16, but 18 if over 125cc.)

A valid UK or Republic of Ireland driving licence is acceptable in **Belgium, Luxembourg** and the **Netherlands**. The minimum age at which a visitor may use a temporarily imported car or motorcycle is 18 for Belgium and the Netherlands and 17 for Luxembourg.

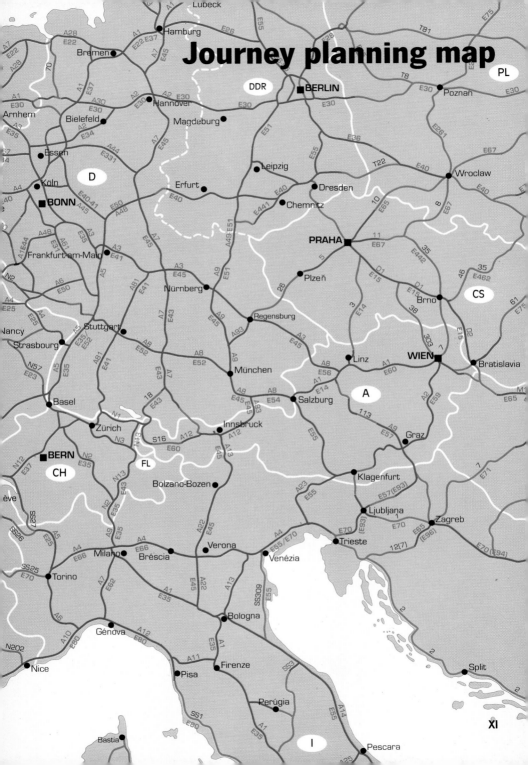

Journey planning map

Map pages

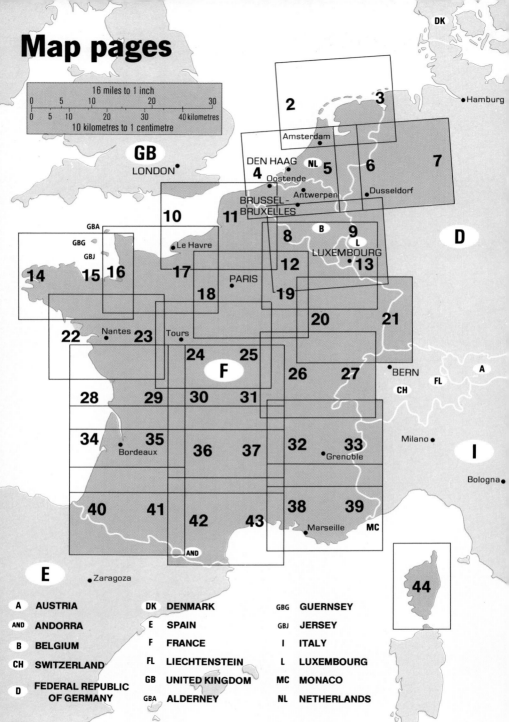

16 miles to 1 inch

0   5   10   20   30

0   5   10   20   30   40 kilometres

10 kilometres to 1 centimetre

GB

LONDON

DK

Hamburg

2   **3**

Amsterdam

DEN HAAG   **NL 5**   **6**   **7**

4   Oostende

BRUSSEL-   Antwerpen   Dusseldorf
BRUXELLES

10   **11**

GBA   **8**   **B**   **9**   **D**

GBG   Le Havre   **L**

GBJ   **17**   LUXEMBOURG

14   **15**   **16**   **12**   **13**

PARIS

18   **19**

20   **21**

22   Nantes   **23**   Tours

24   **25**

F   **26**   **27**   BERN   **A**

28   **29**   **30**   **31**   CH   FL

34   **35**   Milano

Bordeaux   **36**   **37**   **32**   **33**   **I**

Grenoble

Bologna

40   **41**   **38**   **39**

42   **43**   Marseille   **MC**

AND

E   Zaragoza   **44**

A AUSTRIA	**DK** DENMARK	**GBG** GUERNSEY
AND ANDORRA	**E** SPAIN	**GBJ** JERSEY
B BELGIUM	**F** FRANCE	**I** ITALY
CH SWITZERLAND	**FL** LIECHTENSTEIN	**L** LUXEMBOURG
D FEDERAL REPUBLIC OF GERMANY	**GB** UNITED KINGDOM	**MC** MONACO
	GBA ALDERNEY	**NL** NETHERLANDS

Map symbols

A4	Motorway - dual carriageway
A7	Motorway - single carriageway
A1	Toll motorway - dual carriageway
A6	Toll motorway - single carriageway
	Motorway junction
	Motorway junction - restricted access
	Motorway service area
	Motorway under construction
	Primary route
	Main road
	Secondary road
	Other road
D600 E57 N59	Road numbers
	Dual carriageway or four lanes
	Road in poor condition
	Scotland: narrow A roads with passing places
	Under construction
TOLL Toll	Toll road
	Transit route (G.D.R)
	Scenic route
)========(	Road tunnel
	Car transporter (rail)

68	Distances (distances in GB & Ireland are in miles elsewhere in Europe in kilometres)
10·6 970	Mountain pass (height in metres) with closure period
<<	Gradient 14% and over. Arrow points uphill
<	Gradient 6% - 13% Gradient 20% and over in G.B.
	Frontier crossing with restricted opening hours
	Frontier posts
AA	AA shop
AA	AA port shop
IBIZA	Vehicle ferry
	Hovercraft ferry
	Airport
	International boundary
	National boundary
	Viewpoint
	Motor racing circuit
3560 SNOWDON	Mountain/spot height (heights in G.B. and Ireland in feet elsewhere in Europe in metres)
	Mountain railway
	Urban area
	River, lake and canal
Kukkola Rapids	Place of interest
8	Overlaps and numbers of continuing pages

1

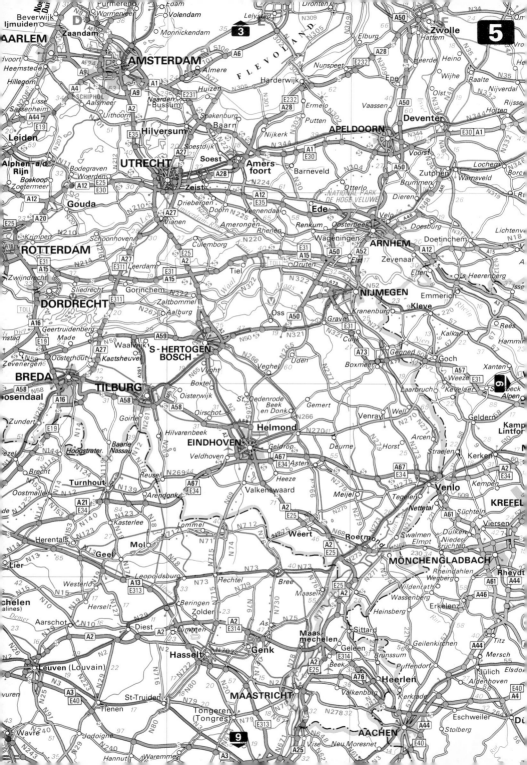

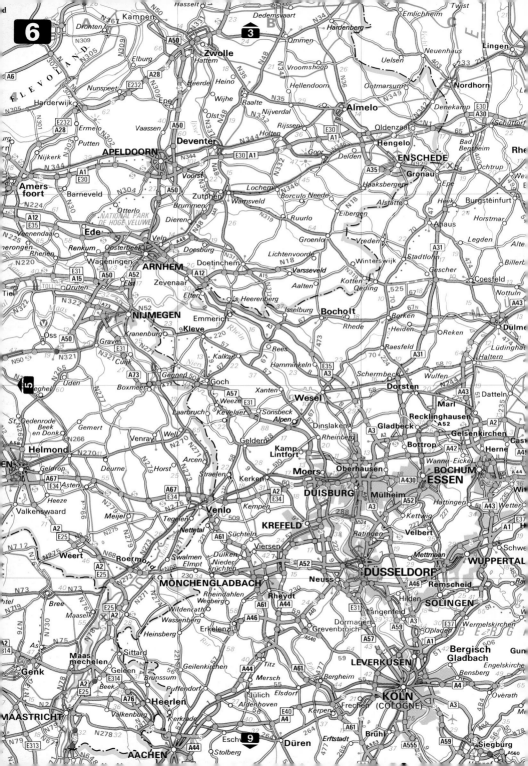

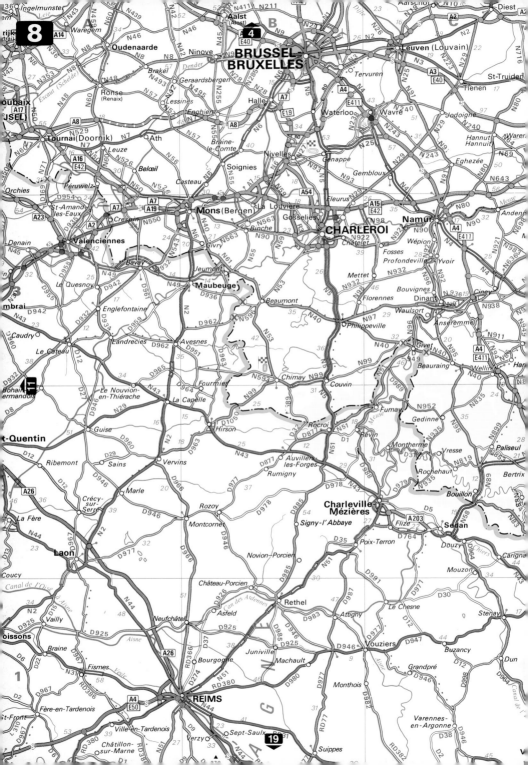

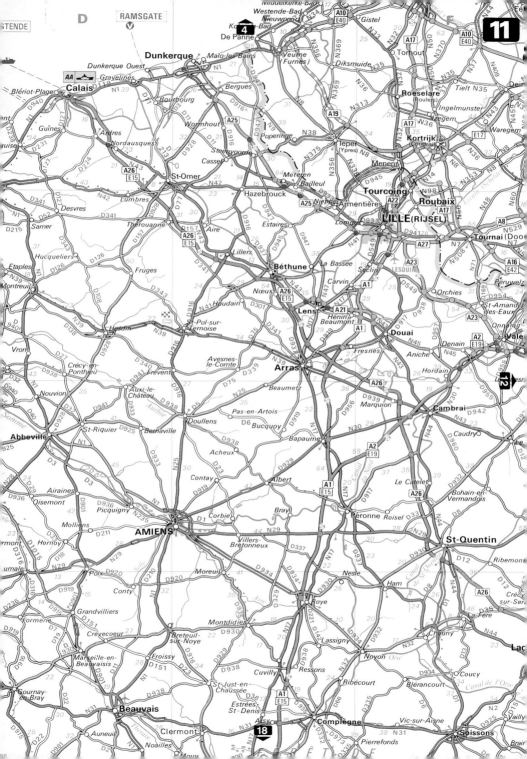

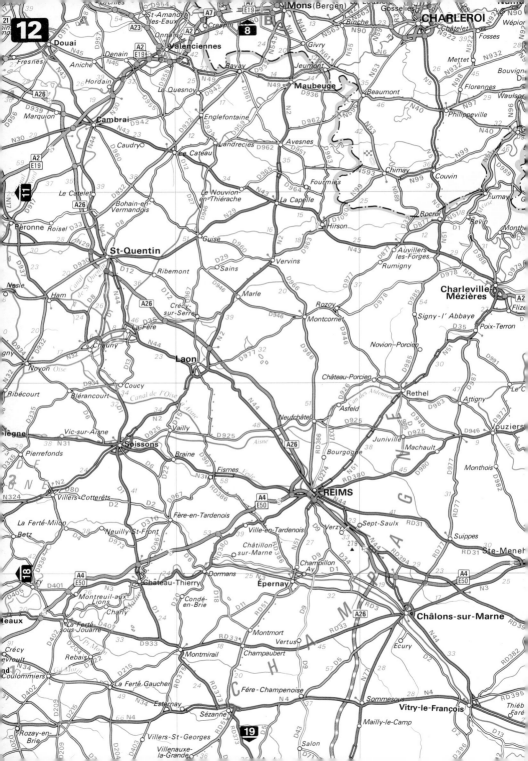

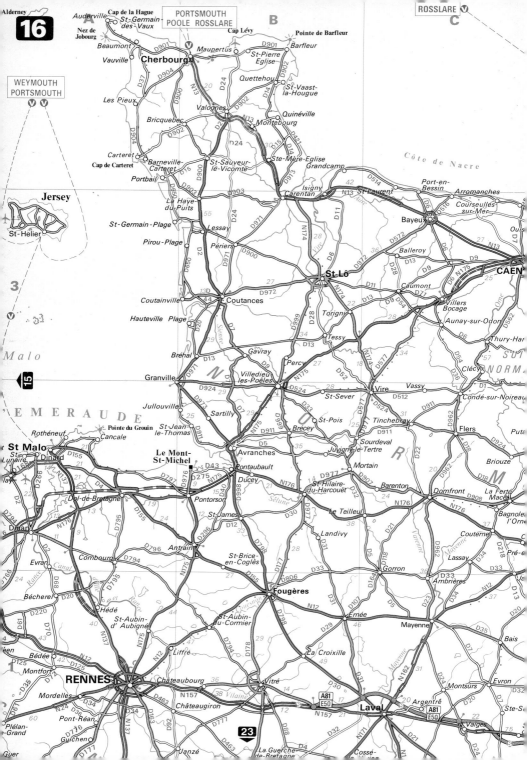

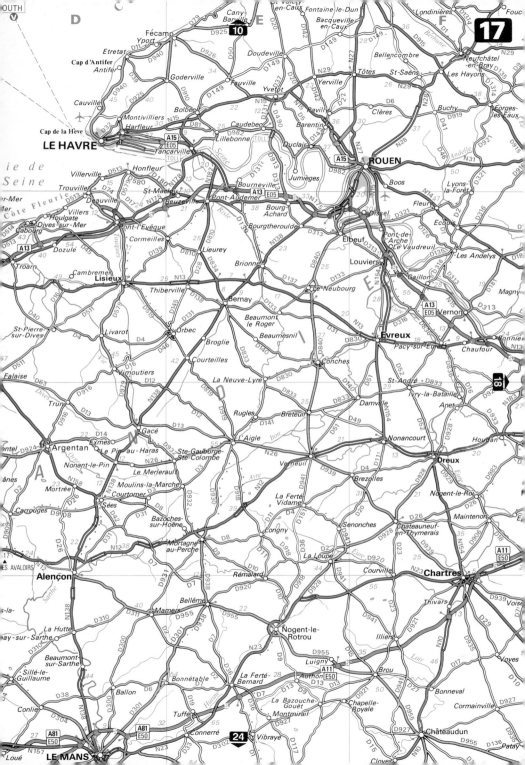

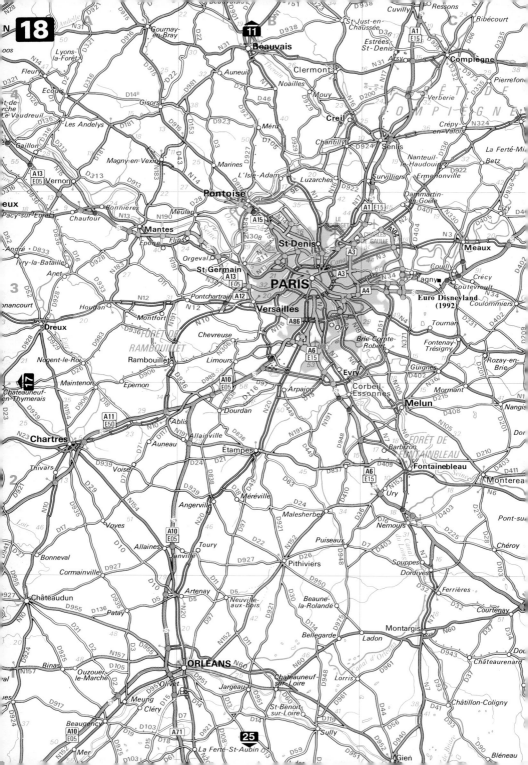

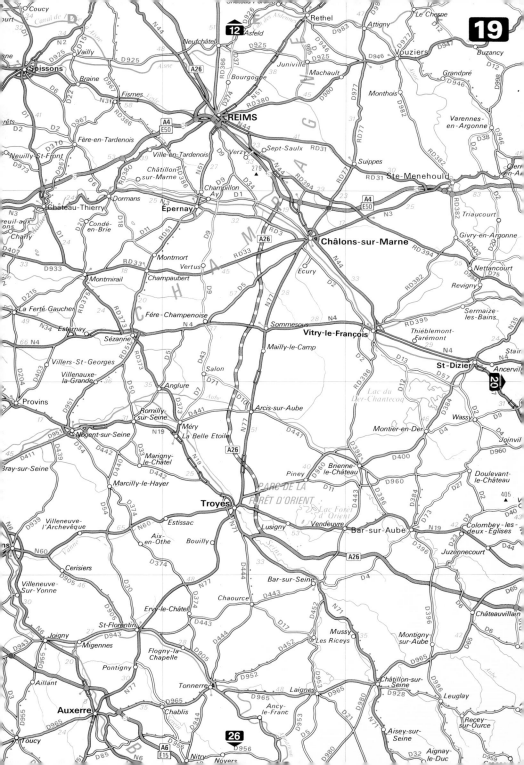

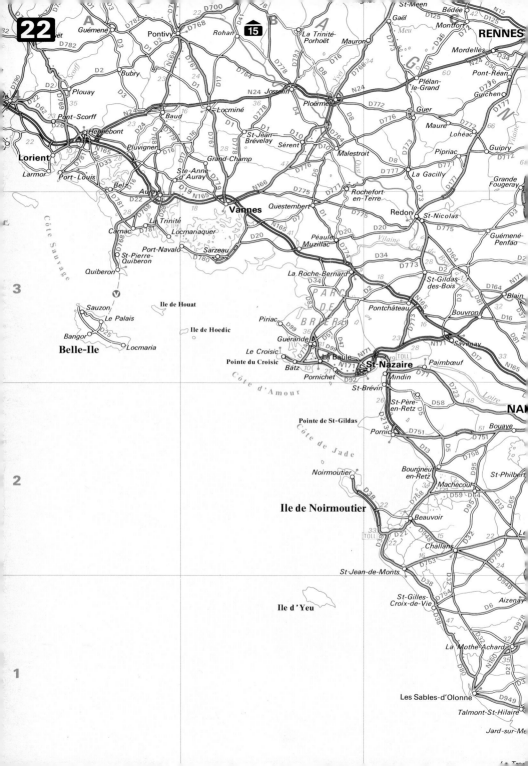

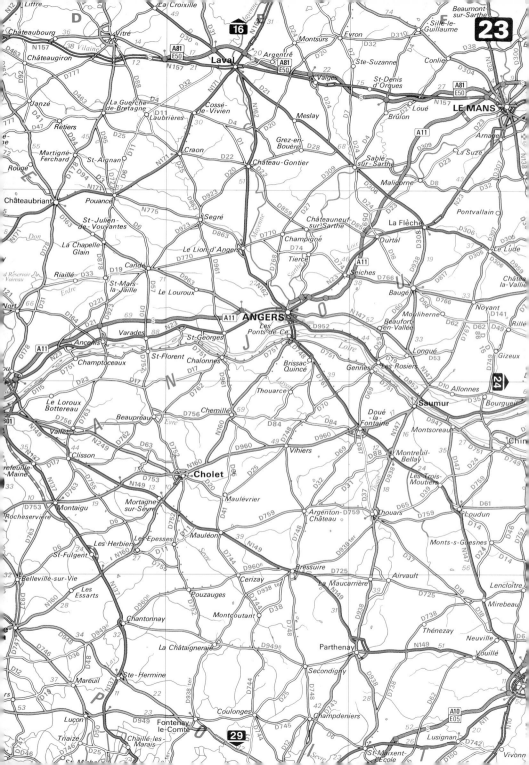

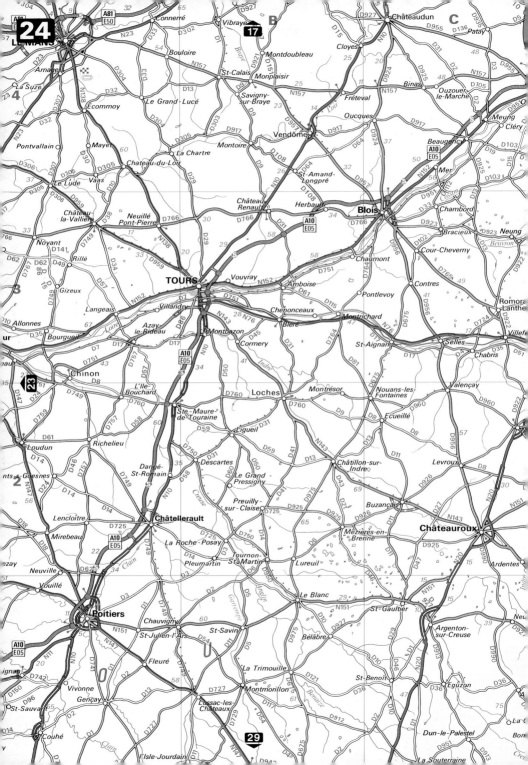

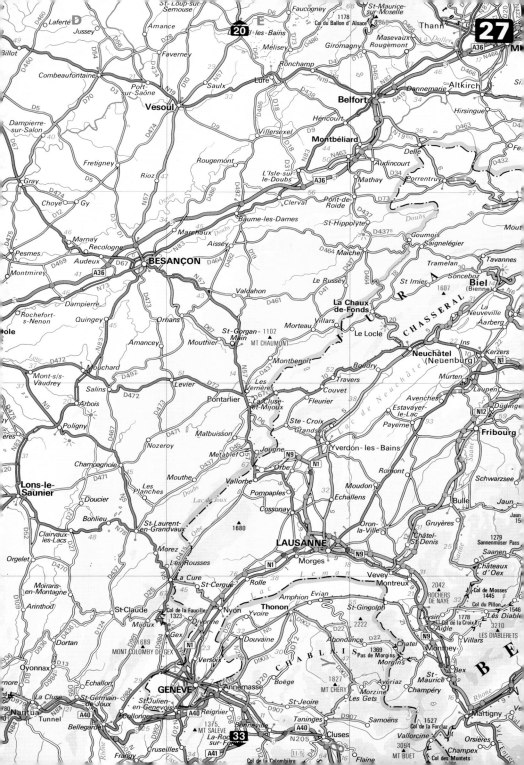

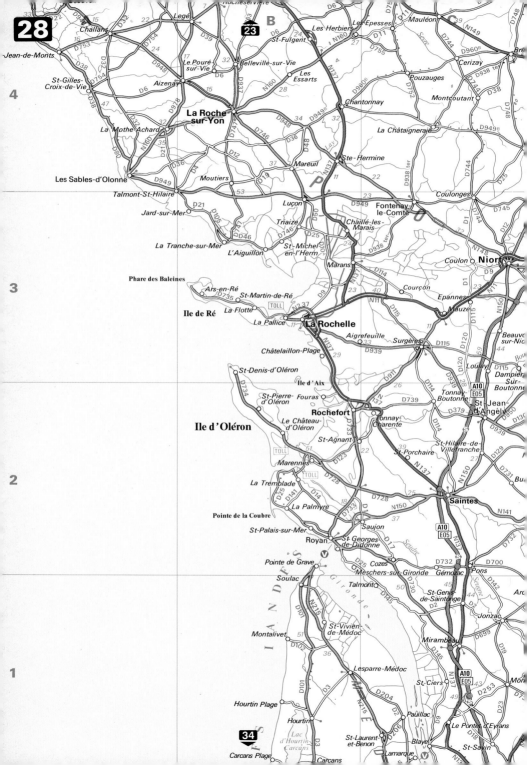

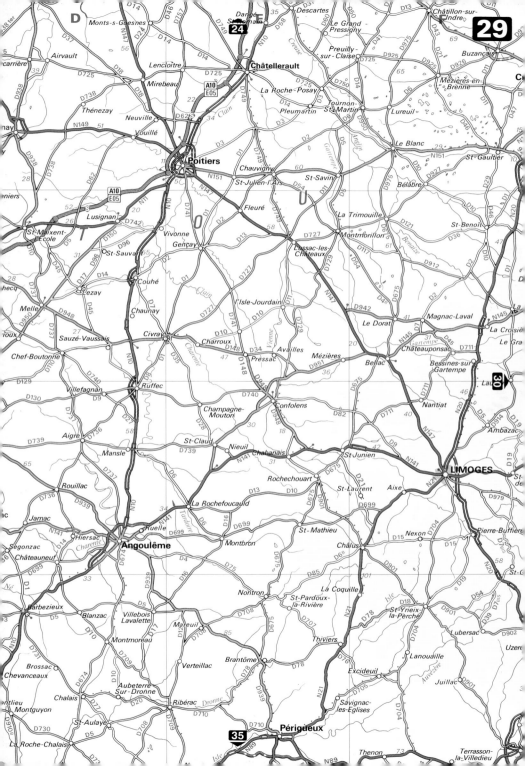

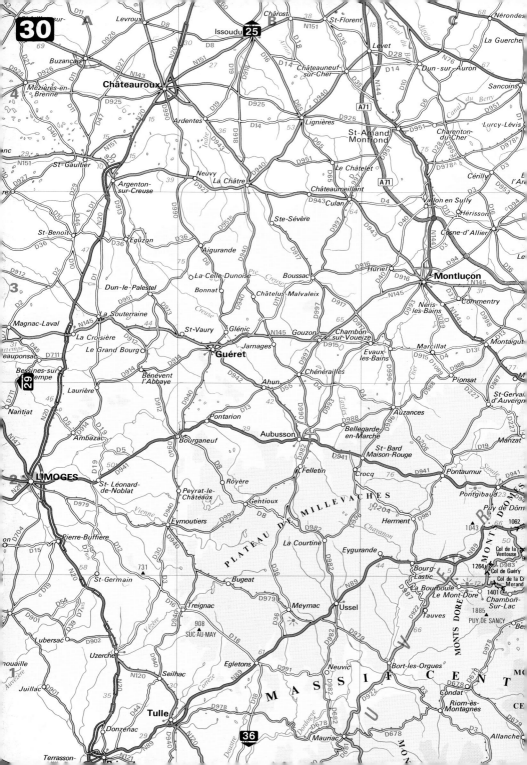

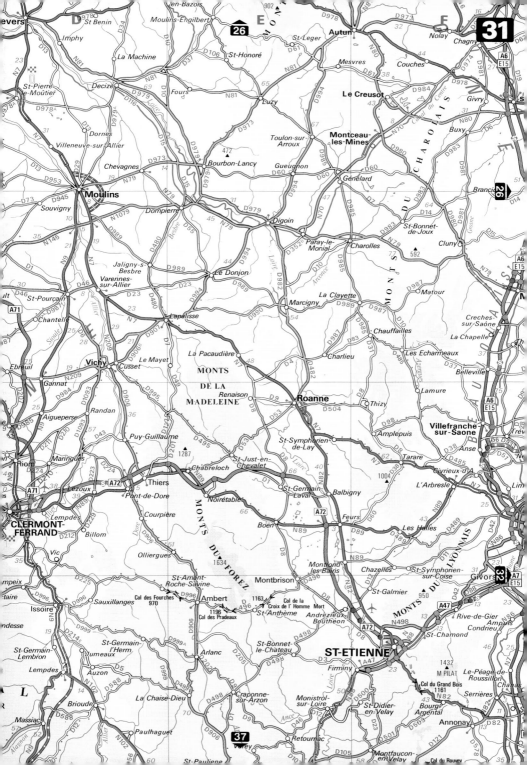

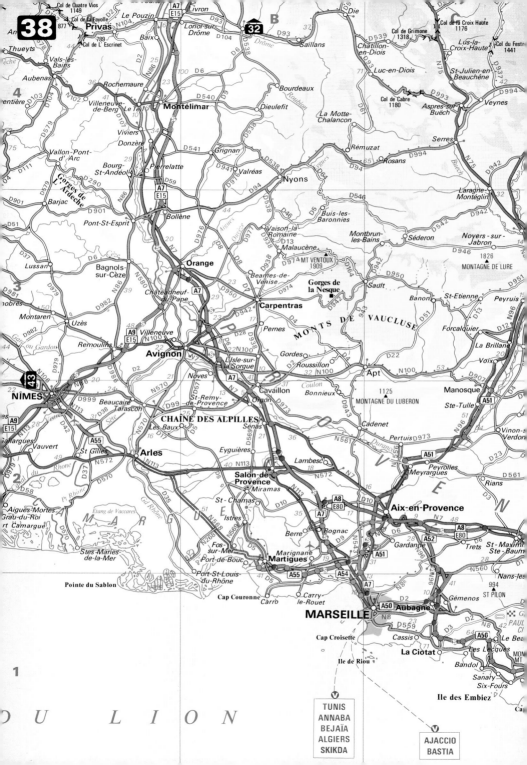

Corse

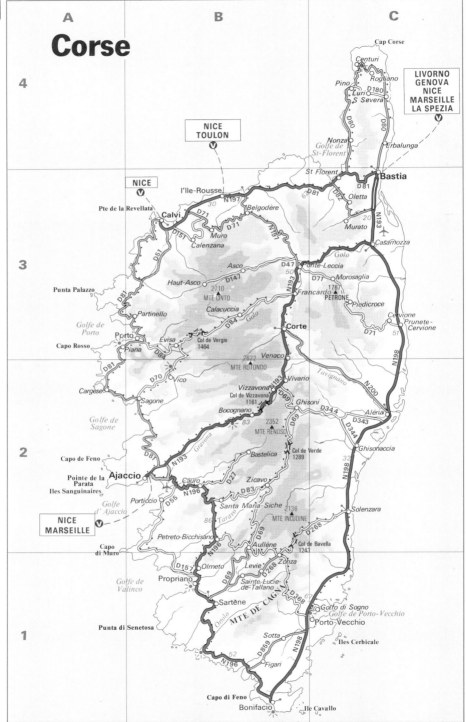

A   **B**   **C**

Cap Corse

**LIVORNO
GENOVA
NICE
MARSEILLE
LA SPEZIA**

Centuri

Rogliano

Pino   D180

Luri

S Severa

**NICE
TOULON**

Nonza

Erbalunga

Golfe de
St-Florent

St Florent

NICE

l'Ile-Rousse

N197   30

Bastia

D81

Oletta

Pte de la Revellata

Calvi

D71

Belgodère

D81

D83

Murato

N193

Muro

D71

D157

Calenzana

Casamozza

Asco

D47   Ponte-Leccia

Golo

Haut-Asco

D147

50

D71

Morosaglia

Punta Palazzo

D81

2710

MTE CINTO

N193   Francardo

1767

PETRONE

Piedicroce

Partinello

Calacuccia

D84   Golo

Cervione

Prunete-
Cervione

Golfe de
Porto

Porto

Evisa

Col de Vergio
1464

Corte

D71

51

N198

Capo Rosso

Piana

D84

2622

Venaco

MTE ROTONDO

Tavignano

Cargèse

D81

D70

Vico

Vivario

Sagone

Vizzavona

N193

Ghisoni

D344

Aléria

Golfe de
Sagone

Col de Vizzavona
1161

D69

Bocognano

83

2352

D343

MTE RENOSO

D344

Ghisonaccia

Capo de Feno

D81

N193

Bastelica

Col de Verde
1289

32

N198

Pointe de la
Parata

Ajaccio

Cauro

D27

Zicavo

Iles Sanguinaires

N196

D83

Solenzara

Porticcio

D55

Santa Maria-Siche

2136

MTE INCUDINE

Golfe
d'Ajaccio

**NICE
MARSEILLE**

Petreto-Bicchisano

N196

Aullène

D69

Col de Bavella
1243

Capo
di Muro

D157

Olmeto

D69

Levie

Zonza

D268

Propriano

Sainte-Lucie-
de-Tallano

67

Golfe de
Valinco

Sartène

MTE DE CAGNA

D268

Golfo di Sogno

Golfe de Porto-Vecchio

Punta di Senetosa

Onno

Porto-Vecchio

Sotta

D859

N198

Iles Cerbicale

52

N196

Figari

Capo di Feno

Bonifacio

Ile Cavallo

Index to place names

To locate a place in the atlas first look up the name in the alphabetical index. The required page number is indicated in bold type. The letter and figure in light type relate to the grid square containing the place on the atlas page. The placename is then found between the intersection of the lines linking the letters (running top and bottom of the page) and the numbers (at the left/right hand-side of the page).

City plans included within the index

Amsterdam	46/47
Antwerpen	48/49
Bordeaux	50/51
Brugge	52
Bruxelles	54/55
Den Haag	56/57
Lille	64/65
Luxembourg	66/67
Lyon	68/69
Marseille	70/71
Nice	72/73
Paris	74/75
Rotterdam	76/77
Strasbourg	78/79

A

Aalburg	5	E3
Aalsmeer	5	D4
Aalst (Alost)	4	C1
Aalten	6	B3
Aalter	4	B2
Aarschot	5	D1
Abbeville	11	D2
Ablis	18	A2
Abondance	27	F1
Abreschviller	21	D3
Abries	33	E1
Accous	40	C2
Acheux	11	E2
Agay	39	E2
Agde	43	D2
Agen	35	E2
Ahun	30	B2
Aignay-le-Duc	26	B4
Aigre	29	D2
Aigrefeuille	28	C3
Aigrefeuille-Sur-Maine	23	D2
Aiguebelle	33	D3
Aiguebelle	39	D1
Aigueperse	31	D2
Aigues-Mortes	43	E3
Aiguilles	33	E1
Aiguillon	35	D2
Aigurande	30	B3
Ailefroide	33	D1
Aillant	25	F4
Aime	33	D3
Ainhoa	40	A2
Airaines	11	D2
Aire	11	E3
Aire-sur-l'Adour	40	C3
Airvault	23	F1
Aisey-sur-Seine	26	B4
Aissey	27	E3
Aisy-sur-Armançon	26	B4
Aixe	29	F2
Aix-en-Othe	19	D2
Aix-en-Provence	38	C2
Aix-les-Bains	32	C3
Aizenay	22	C1
Ajaccio	44	B2
Alban	42	C4
Albens	32	C3
Albert	11	E2
Albertville	33	D3
Albi	42	B4
Alençon	17	D2
Aléria	44	C2
Alès	37	E1
Alkmaar	2	B2
Allaines	18	A2

Allainville	18	B2
Allanche	36	C4
Allemond	32	C2
Allevard	32	C2
Allonnes	23	F2
Allos	39	D3
Almelo	6	B4
Almere	2	C1
Alost (Aalst)	4	C1
Alphen-ann-de-Rijn	5	D4
Altkirch	21	E1
Alvignac	36	A3
Alzon	43	D4
Alzonne	42	B2
Amance	20	C1
Amancey	27	D3
Amay	9	D4
Ambarès	34	C3
Ambazac	30	A2
Ambérieu-en-Bugey	32	B4
Ambert	31	E1
Amboise	24	B3
Ambrières	16	C1
Amélie-les-Bains	42	C1
Amerongen	5	E3
Amersfoort	5	E4
Amiens	11	E2
Amou	40	C3
Amphion	27	E1
Amplepuis	31	F2
Ampuis	32	A2
Amsterdam	2	C1
Ancenis	23	D3
Ancerville	20	A3
Ancy-le-Franc	26	A4
Andelot	20	B2
Andenne	8	C3
Andernos	34	B3
Andijk	2	C2
Andolsheim	21	E2
Andrézieux-Bouthéon	31	E1
Anduze	37	E1
Anet	18	A3
Angers	23	E3
Angerville	18	B2
Anglet	40	A3
Anglure	19	D2
Angoulême	29	D2
Aniane	43	D3
Aniche	12	A4
Anjum	3	D3
Anna Paulowna	2	B2
Annecy	32	C3
Annemasse	33	D4
Annonay	32	A2
Annot	39	E3
Anse	32	A3
Anseremme	8	C3
Anthéor	39	E2
Antibes	39	E2
Antifer	10	A1
Antraigues	37	F3
Antrain	16	B2
Antwerpen (Anvers)	4	C2
Anvers (Antwerpen)	4	C2
Apeldoorn	6	A4
Appingedam	3	E3
Apt	38	C3
Arachon	34	B3
Aramits	40	C2
Arbois	27	D2
Arcen	5	F2
Arc-en-Barrois	20	A2
Arches	21	D2
Archiac	28	C1
Arcis-sur-Aube	19	E2
Ardentes	24	C2
Ardres	11	D4
Arendonk	5	D2
Ares	34	B3
Argancy	13	F2
Argelès-Gazost	41	D2

Argelès-Plage

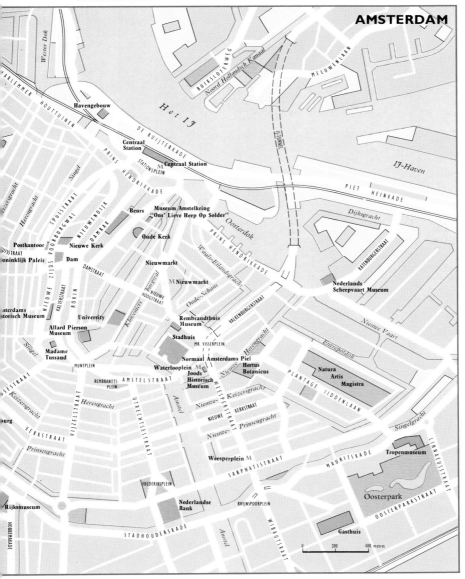

Arras	11	E3
Arreau	41	D2
Arrens	40	C2
Arromanches	16	C3
Ars	13	E2
Ars-en-Ré	28	B3
Arsy	18	C4
Artemare	32	C3
Artenay	18	B1
Artix	40	C3
Arudy	40	C2
Arvieux	33	E1
Arzacq-Arraziguet	40	C3
As	5	E1
Ascain	40	A3
Asco	44	B3
Asfeld	12	B2
Aspet	41	E2
Aspres-sur-Buech	38	C4
Assen	3	E2
Astaffort	35	E1
Asten	5	E2
Ath	8	A4
Attigny	12	C2
Aubagne	38	C1
Aubange	9	D2
Aubenas	37	F2
Auberive	20	A1
Aubeterre-sur-Dronne	35	D4
Aubigny	25	D3
Auboué	13	E2
Aubusson	30	B2
Auch	41	E3
Auderville	16	A4
Audeux	27	D3
Audierne	14	A1
Audincourt	27	F4
Audressein	41	F2
Audun-le-Roman	13	E2
Augenge	34	B3
Aullène	44	B2
Aulnay	28	C2
Ault	10	C2
Aulus-les-Bains	41	F1
Aumale	11	D2
Aumetz	13	E2
Aumont-Aubrac	37	D3
Aunay-sur-Odon	16	C3
Auneau	18	A2
Auneuil	18	B4
Aups	39	D2
Auray	22	A3
Aurignac	41	E2
Aurillac	36	C3
Auron	39	E3
Auterive	42	A3
Authon	17	E1
Autun	26	B2
Auvillers-les-Forges	12	C3
Auxerre	25	F4
Auxi-le-Château	11	D2
Auxonne	26	C3
Auzances	30	C2
Auzon	37	D4
Availles	29	E3
Avallon	26	A4
Avesnes	12	B4
Avesnes-le-Comte	11	E3
Avignon	38	B3
Avoriaz	33	E4
Avranches	16	B2
Axat	42	B1

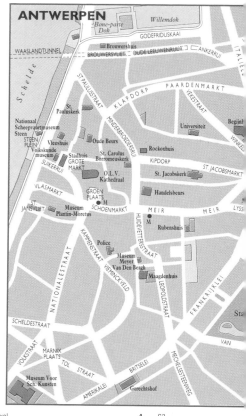

Axel	4	C2
Ax-les-Thermes	42	B1
Ay	19	E3
Azay-le-Rideau	24	A3

B

Baale Nassau	5	D2
Baarn	5	E4
Baccarat	21	D3
Bacqueville-en-Caux	10	C2
Badonviller	21	D3
Bagnères-de-Bigorre	41	D2
Bagnères-de-Luchon	41	E1
Bagnoles-de-l'Orne	16	C2
Bagnols-en-Forêt	39	E2
Bagnols-les-Bains	37	E2
Bagnols-sur-Cèze	38	A3
Baigneux-les-Juifs	26	B4
Bailleul	11	E4
Bain-de-Bretagne	22	C4
Bains-les-Bains	20	C2
Bais	16	C1
Baix	32	A1
Baixas	42	C1

Balbigny

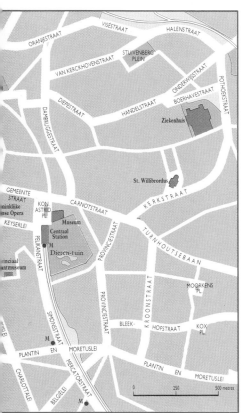

Bastelica	**44**	B2
Bastia	**44**	C4
Bastogne	**9**	D2
Battice	**9**	D4
Batz	**22**	B3
Baud	**22**	A4
Baugé	**23**	F3
Baugy	**25**	E2
Baume-les-Dames	**27**	E3
Bavay	**12**	B4
Bayeux	**16**	C3
Bayon	**20**	C3
Bayonne	**40**	A3
Bazas	**35**	D2
Bazoches-sur-Hoëne	**17**	E2
Beaucaire	**38**	A2
Beaufort	**33**	D3
Beaufort-en-Vallée	**23**	F3
Beaugency	**24**	C4
Beaulieu	**39**	F2
Beaulieu-sur-Dordogne	**36**	B3
Beaumes-de-Venise	**38**	B3
Beaumesnil	**17**	E3
Beaumetz	**11**	E2
Beaumont	**16**	A4
Beaumont	**35**	E3
Beaumont	**8**	B3
Beaumont-de-Lomagne	**41**	F4
Beaumont le Roger	**17**	E3
Beaumont-sur-Sarthe	**17**	D1
Beaune	**26**	C3
Beaune-la-Rolande	**18**	B1
Beaupréau	**23**	D2
Beauraing	**8**	C3
Beaurepaire	**32**	B2
Beaurepaire-en-Bresse	**26**	C2
Beauvais	**11**	D1
Beauvallon	**39**	E1
Beauvezer	**39**	D3
Beauvoir	**22**	C2
Beauvoir-sur-Niort	**28**	C3
Bécherel	**15**	E2
Bédarieux	**43**	D3
Bédée	**15**	E1
Bedous	**40**	C2
Beek	**5**	E1
Beek en Donk	**5**	E2
Bégard	**14**	C3
Beg-Meil	**14**	B1
Beilen	**3**	E2
Bélâbre	**29**	F4
Belcaire	**42**	B1
Belfort	**27**	F4
Belgodère	**44**	B3
Belin-Béliet	**34**	C2
Bellac	**29**	F3
Bellegarde	**18**	B1
Bellegarde	**32**	C4
Bellegarde-en-Marche	**30**	B2
Belle-Isle-en-Terre	**14**	C2
Bellême	**17**	E1
Bellencombre	**10**	C1
Belleville	**32**	A4
Belleville-sur-Vie	**23**	D1
Belley	**32**	C3
Belmont-sur-Rance	**42**	C4
Belœil	**8**	A4
Belvès	**35**	F3
Belz	**22**	A4
Bénévent l'Abbaye	**30**	A3
Benfeld	**21**	E3
Bénodet	**14**	B1

Balbigny	**31**	E2
Balleroy	**16**	C3
Ballon	**17**	D1
Bandol	**38**	C1
Bangor	**22**	A3
Bannalec	**14**	B1
Banon	**38**	C3
Banyuls	**43**	D1
Bapaume	**11**	E2
Baraqueville	**36**	C2
Barbaste	**35**	D1
Barbezieux	**29**	D1
Barbizon	**18**	C2
Barbotan	**41**	D4
Barcelonnette	**39**	E4
Barentin	**17**	E4
Barenton	**16**	C2
Barfleur	**16**	B4
Barjac	**37**	F2
Barjols	**39**	D2
Bar-le-Duc	**20**	B3
Barneveld	**5**	E4
Barneville-Carteret	**16**	A4
Barr	**21**	E3
Barre-des-Cévennes	**37**	E2
Barrême	**39**	D3
Bar-sur-Aube	**19**	F2
Bar-sur-Seine	**19**	E1

Berck-Plage	**10**	C3
Bergen (Mons)	**8**	B3
Bergen	**2**	B2
Bergen aan Zee	**2**	B2
Bergen op Zoom	**4**	C2
Bergerac	**35**	E3
Bergues	**11**	E4
Bergum	**3**	D3
Beringen	**5**	E1
Bernaville	**11**	D2
Bernay	**17**	E3
Berres	**38**	B2
Bertrix	**8**	C2
Besançon	**27**	D3
Bessan	**43**	D3
Besse-en-Chandesse	**30**	C1
Besse-sur-Issole	**39**	D2
Bessines-sur-Gartempe	**30**	A3
Béthune	**11**	E3
Betz	**18**	C4
Beuil	**39**	E3
Beuzeville	**17**	D3
Beveren-Waas	**4**	C2
Beverwijk	**2**	B1
Beynac-et-Cazenac	**35**	F3
Beynat	**36**	A3
Béziers	**43**	D3
Biarritz	**40**	A3
Bias	**34**	B2
Bidache	**40**	B3
Bidart	**40**	A3
Bierre-Lès-Semur	**26**	B3
Billom	**31**	D2
Binas	**18**	A1
Binche	**8**	B3
Binic	**15**	D2
Biscarrosse	**34**	B2
Biscarrosse-Plage	**34**	B2
Bitche	**21**	E4
Blain	**22**	C3
Blâmont	**21**	D3
Blangy	**11**	D2
Blankenberge	**4**	B2
Blanzac	**29**	D1
Blaye	**34**	C4
Bléneau	**25**	E4
Blérancourt	**11**	F1
Bléré	**24**	B3
Blériot-Plage	**11**	D4
Bletterans	**27**	D2
Bligny	**26**	B3
Blois	**24**	C3
Blokzijl	**3**	D2
Bocognano	**44**	B2
Bodegraven	**5**	D4
Boëge	**27**	E1
Boën	**31**	E2
Bohain-en-Vermandois	**12**	A3
Bolbec	**10**	B1
Bollène	**38**	A3
Bologne	**20**	B2
Bolsward	**3**	D2
Bonifacio	**44**	B1
Bonlieu	**27**	D2
Bonnat	**30**	B3
Bonnétable	**17**	D1
Bonneval	**17**	F1
Bonneval	**33**	E2
Bonneville	**33**	D4
Bonnières	**18**	A3
Bonnieux	**38**	B2
Bonny-sur-Loire	**25**	E3

Boom	**4**	C1
Boos	**17**	F4
Borculo	**6**	B3
Bordeaux	**34**	C3
Bordères	**41**	D1
Borger	**3**	E2
Bormes-les-Mimosas	**39**	D1
Bort-les-Orgues	**30**	C1
Boskoop	**5**	D4
Bouaye	**22**	C2
Bouillon	**8**	C2
Bouilly	**19**	E2
Boulay-Moselle	**13**	F2
Boulogne-sur-Gesse	**41**	E2
Boulogne-sur-Mer	**11**	D4
Bouloire	**24**	A4
Bourbon Lancy	**26**	A2
Bourbon-l'Archambault	**31**	D4

50

Bourbonne-les-Bains

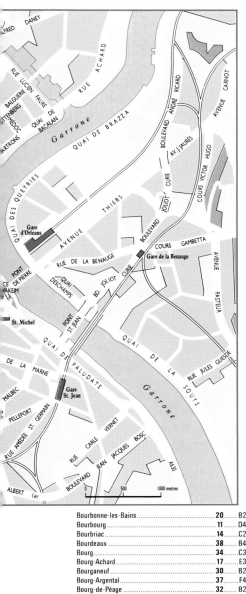

Bourgtheroulde .... **17** E3
Bourgueil .... **24** A3
Bourmont .... **20** B2
Bourneville .... **17** E4
Boussac .... **30** B3
Boussens .... **41** E2
Bouvignes .... **8** C3
Bouvron .... **22** C3
Bouxwiller .... **21** E4
Bouzonville .... **13** F2
Boxmeer .... **5** F3
Boxtel .... **5** E2
Bozel .... **33** D3
Bracieux .... **24** C3
Braine .... **12** A2
Braine-le-Comte .... **8** B4
Brakel .... **4** B1
Brancion .... **26** B2
Branne .... **35** D3
Brantôme .... **35** E4
Brassac .... **42** C3
Brasschaat .... **5** D2
Bray .... **11** E2
Bray-sur-Seine .... **19** D2
Brécey .... **16** B2
Brecht .... **5** D2
Breda .... **5** D3
Bredene .... **4** A2
Bree .... **5** E1
Bréhal .... **16** B3
Breil-sur-Roya .... **39** F3
Breskens .... **4** B2
Bressuire .... **23** E2
Brest .... **14** A2
Bretenoux .... **36** B3
Breteuil .... **17** E2
Breteuil-sur-Noye .... **11** D1
Brezolles .... **17** F2
Briançon .... **33** D1
Briare .... **25** E3
Bricquebec .... **16** B4
Briec .... **14** B2
Brie-Comte-Robert .... **18** C3
Brielle .... **4** C3
Brienne-le-Château .... **19** F2
Briey .... **13** E2
Brignogan .... **14** A3
Brignoles .... **39** D2
Brignoud .... **32** C2
Brionne .... **17** E3
Brioude .... **37** D4
Brioux .... **29** D3
Briouze .... **16** C2
Brissac-Quincé .... **23** E3
Brive-la-Gaillarde .... **36** A3
Broglie .... **17** E3
Broons .... **15** E2
Brossac .... **35** D4
Brou .... **17** F1
Brouvelieures .... **21** D2
Brouwershaven .... **4** C3
Brugge .... **4** B2
Brûlon .... **23** F4
Brumath .... **21** E3
Brummen .... **6** B3
Bruniquel .... **36** A1
Brunssum .... **5** F1
Brussel (Bruxelles) .... **4** C1
Bruxelles (Brussel) .... **4** C1
Bruyères .... **21** D2
Bubry .... **14** C1
Buchy .... **10** C1

Bourbonne-les-Bains .... **20** B2
Bourbourg .... **11** D4
Bourbriac .... **14** C2
Bourdeaux .... **38** B4
Bourg .... **34** C3
Bourg-Achard .... **17** E3
Bourganeuf .... **30** B2
Bourg-Argental .... **37** F4
Bourg-de-Péage .... **32** B2
Bourg-en-Bresse .... **32** B4
Bourges .... **25** D2
Bourg-Lastic .... **30** C2
Bourg-Madame .... **42** B1
Bourgneuf-en-Retz .... **22** C2
Bourgogne .... **12** B2
Bourgoin-Jallieu .... **32** B3
Bourg-St-Andéol .... **38** A4
Bourg-St-Maurice .... **33** E3

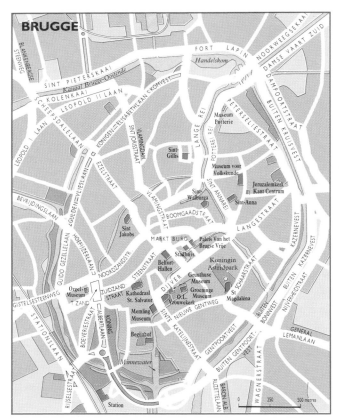

Bucquoy	11	E2
Bugeat	30	B1
Buis-les-Baronnies	38	B3
Buitenpost	3	D3
Bulgnéville	20	C2
Burgh-Haamstede	4	B3
Burie	28	C2
Bussang	21	D1
Bussum	5	E4
Butgenbach	9	E3
Buxy	26	B2
Buzançais	24	C2
Buzancy	13	D2

Calais	11	D4
Calenzana	44	B3
Calignac	35	E1
Callac	14	C2
Calvi	44	B3
Camarès	42	C4
Camaret	14	A2
Cambo-les-Bains	40	A3
Cambrai	12	A4
Cambremer	17	D3
Campan	41	D2
Cancale	15	E3
Cancon	35	E2
Candé	23	D3
Canet-Plage	43	D1
Cannes	39	E2
Cany-Barville	10	B2
Capbreton	40	A3
Cap-d'Ail	39	F2
Capendu	42	C2
Capestang	43	D2
Cap Ferret	34	B3
Cap Gris Nez	11	D4
Captieux	34	C2
Caraman	42	A3
Carantec	14	C3
Carbon-Blanc	34	C3
Carbonne	41	F2

C

Cabourg	17	D3
Cabrerets	36	A2
Cadenet	38	B2
Cadillac	34	C2
Caen	16	C3
Cagnes	39	E2
Cahors	36	A2
Cajarc	36	B2
Calacuccia	44	B3

Carcans	34	B3	Chalamont	32	B4
Carcans Plage	34	B3	Chalampé	21	E1
Carcassonne	42	B2	Challans	22	C2
Carcès	39	D2	Challes-les-Eaux	32	C3
Carennac	36	A3	Chalonnes	23	E3
Carenton	16	B3	Châlons-sur-Marne	19	E3
Cargèse	44	A2	Chalon-sur-Saône	26	C2
Carhaix-Plouguer	14	C2	Châlus	29	F2
Carignan	13	D3	Chambéry	32	C3
Carling	13	F2	Chambley	13	E2
Carmaux	36	B1	Chambon-sur-Lac	30	C1
Carnac	22	A3	Chambon-sur-Voueize	30	C3
Carpentras	38	B3	Chambord	24	C3
Carquefou	23	D3	Chamonix	33	E4
Carqueiranne	39	D1	Champagne-Mouton	29	E2
Carro	38	B1	Champagnole	27	D2
Carrouges	17	D2	Champaubert	19	D3
Carry-le-Rouet	38	B1	Champdeniers	28	C3
Carteret	16	A4	Champeix	31	D1
Carvin	11	E3	Champier	32	B2
Casamozza	44	C3	Champigné	23	E3
Cassagnes-Bégonhès	36	C1	Champillon	12	B2
Cassel	11	E4	Champlitte	27	D4
Cassis	38	C1	Champlon	9	D3
Casteau	8	B4	Champtoceaux	23	D3
Casteljaloux	35	D2	Chanas	32	A2
Castellane	39	D3	Chantelle	31	D3
Castelmoron	35	E2	Chantemerle	33	D1
Castelnaudary	42	B2	Chantilly	18	B4
Castelnau-de-Médoc	34	C3	Chantonnay	23	D1
Castelnau-de-Montmiral	42	B4	Chaource	19	E1
Castelnau-Magnoac	41	E2	Chapelle-Royale	17	E1
Castelsarrasin	41	F4	Charavines	32	C2
Castets	40	B4	Charenton-sur-Cher	25	E2
Castillon-la-Bataille	35	D3	Charleroi	8	B3
Castillonnès	35	E2	Charleville-Mézières	12	C3
Castres	42	B3	Charlieu	31	E3
Castricum	2	B1	Charly	19	D3
Castries	43	E3	Charmes	20	C2
Catus	35	F2	Charny	25	E4
Caudebec	17	E4	Charolles	31	E3
Caudry	12	A4	Chârost	25	D2
Caumont	16	C3	Charroux	29	E3
Caunes	42	C2	Chartres	18	A2
Cauro	44	B2	Chassigny	20	B1
Caussade	36	A1	Château-Arnoux	38	C3
Cauterets	41	D1	Châteaubourg	16	B1
Cauville	10	A1	Châteaubriant	23	D3
Cavaillon	38	B2	Château-Chinon	26	A3
Cavalaire-sur-Mer	39	D1	Château-du-Loir	24	A4
Cavalière	39	D1	Châteaudun	17	F1
Caylus	36	A2	Châteaugiron	23	D4
Cazals	35	F2	Château-Gontier	23	E4
Cazères	41	F2	Château-la-Vallière	24	A3
Centuri	44	C4	Châteaulin	14	B2
Cerbere	43	D1	Châteaumeillant	30	B3
Céret	42	C1	Châteauneuf	29	D2
Cérilly	30	C4	Châteauneuf-de-Faou	14	B2
Cerisiers	19	D2	Châteauneuf-de-Randon	37	E2
Cerizay	23	E2	Châteauneuf-du-Pape	38	B3
Cernay	21	E1	Châteauneuf-en-Thymerais	17	F2
Cervione	44	C3	Châteauneuf-sur-Cher	25	D2
Ceyzériat	32	B4	Châteauneuf-sur-Loire	25	D4
Chabanais	29	E2	Châteauneuf-sur-Sarthe	23	E3
Chabeuil	32	B1	Châteauponsac	29	F3
Chablis	26	A4	Château-Porcien	12	C3
Chabreloch	31	E2	Château-Queyras	33	E1
Chabris	24	C3	Châteaurenard	18	C1
Chagny	26	B2	Château-Renault	24	B3
Chaillé-les-Marais	28	B3	Châteauroux	24	C2
Chalabre	42	B2	Château-Salins	21	D3
Chalais	35	D4	Château-Thierry	19	D3

Châteauvillain	20	A2
Chatel	27	F1
Châtelaillon-Plage	28	B3
Châtelet	8	B3
Châtelguyon	31	D2
Châtellerault	24	A2
Châtelus-Malvaleix	30	B3
Châtenois	20	C2
Châtillon-Coligny	25	E4
Châtillon-en-Bazois	25	F2
Châtillon-en-Diois	32	C1
Châtillon-sur-Chalaronne	32	B4
Châtillon-sur-Indre	24	B2
Châtillon-sur-Loire	25	E3
Châtillon-sur-Marne	12	B2
Châtillon-sur-Seine	19	F1
Chaudes-Aigues	37	D3
Chauffailles	31	F3
Chaufour	18	A3
Chaumergy	27	D2
Chaumont	20	B2
Chaumont	24	B3
Chaunay	29	D3
Chauny	12	A3
Chaussin	26	C3
Chauvigny	29	E4
Chazelles	31	F2
Chef-Boutonne	29	D3
Chemillé	23	E2
Chemin	26	C3
Chénérailles	30	B3
Chenonceaux	24	B3
Cherbourg	16	B4
Chéroy	18	C2
Chevagnes	31	D4
Chevanceaux	35	D4
Chevreuse	18	B3
Chimay	8	B3
Chinon	24	A3
Cholêt	23	E2
Chorges	39	D4
Choye	27	D3
Ciboure	40	A3
Cierp	41	E2
Ciney	8	C3
Cintegabelle	42	A2
Cirey	21	D3
Civraux	29	D3
Civrieux-d'A.	32	A3
Clairvaux-les-Lacs	27	D2
Clamecy	25	F3
Clavière	33	E1
Clécy	16	C3
Clefmont	20	B2
Clelles	32	C1
Clères	10	C1
Clermont	18	B4
Clermont-en-Argonne	13	D2
Clermont-Ferrand	31	D2
Clermont-l'Hérault	43	D3
Clerval	27	E3
Clervaux	9	E2
Cléry	24	C4
Clisson	23	D2
Cloyes	24	B4
Cluny	26	B2
Cluses	33	D4
Coevorden	3	E2
Cognac	28	C2
Cogolin	39	D1
Coligny	26	C1
Collinée	15	D2

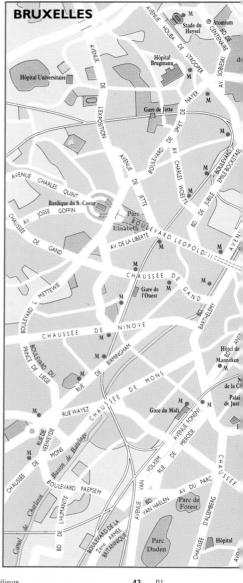

BRUXELLES

Collioure	43	D1
Collonges	32	C4
Colmar	21	E2
Colmars	39	D3
Cologne	41	E3
Colombey-les-Belles	20	C3
Colombey-les-deux-Eglises	20	A2
Combeaufontaine	20	C1
Combourg	15	E2
Combronde	31	D2

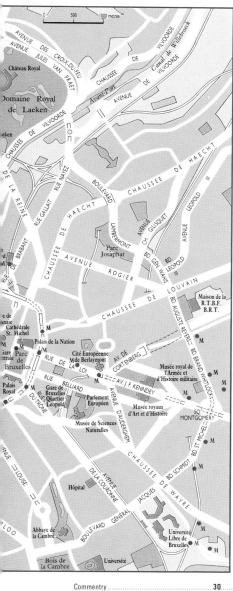

Commentry	**30**	C3
Commercy	**20**	B3
Compiègne	**18**	C4
Comps-sur-Artuby	**39**	D2
Concarneau	**14**	B1
Conches	**17**	E3
Condat	**36**	C4
Condé-en-Brie	**19**	D3
Condé-sur-Noireau	**16**	C2
Condom	**41**	D4

Condrieu	**32**	A2
Conflans	**13**	E2
Confolens	**29**	E2
Conlie	**17**	D1
Connerré	**17**	E1
Conques	**36**	C2
Contay	**11**	E2
Contres	**24**	C3
Contrexéville	**20**	C2
Conty	**11**	D1
Coray	**14**	B1
Corbeil-Essonnes	**18**	B2
Corbie	**11**	E2
Corbigny	**26**	A3
Corcieux	**21**	D2
Cordes	**36**	B1
Corlay	**14**	C2
Cormainville	**18**	A2
Cormeilles	**17**	E3
Cormery	**24**	B3
Cornimont	**21**	D2
Corps	**32**	C1
Corte	**44**	B3
Cosne	**25**	E3
Cosne d'Allier	**30**	C3
Cossé-le-Vivien	**23**	E4
Cotignac	**39**	D2
Couches	**26**	B2
Coucy	**12**	A2
Couhé	**29**	D3
Couilly	**18**	C3
Couiza	**42**	B2
Coulommiers	**18**	C3
Coulon	**28**	C3
Coulonges	**28**	C3
Couptrain	**16**	C2
Courcheval	**33**	D2
Cour-Cheverny	**24**	C3
Courçon	**28**	C3
Courpière	**31**	D2
Courseulles-sur-Mer	**16**	C3
Courson-les-Carrières	**25**	F4
Courteilles	**17**	E3
Courtenay	**18**	C1
Courtomer	**17**	D2
Courtrai (Kortrijk)	**4**	B1
Courville	**17**	F2
Coutainville	**16**	B3
Coutances	**16**	B3
Couterne	**16**	C2
Coutevroult	**18**	C3
Coutras	**35**	D3
Couvin	**8**	B3
Cozes	**28**	C2
Craon	**23**	E4
Craponne-sur-Arzon	**37**	E4
Creches-sur-Saône	**32**	A4
Crécy	**18**	C3
Crécy-en-Ponthieu	**11**	D3
Crécy-sur-Serre	**12**	B3
Creil	**18**	B4
Crémieu	**32**	B3
Créon	**34**	C3
Crépy-en-Valois	**18**	C4
Crespin	**12**	B4
Cressensac	**36**	A3
Crest	**32**	B1
Creutzwald	**13**	F2
Crèvecœur	**11**	D1
Crocq	**30**	B2
Crozon	**14**	A2
Cruseilles	**32**	C4

Cruzy	**42**	C3
Cuers	**39**	D1
Cuijk	**5**	F3
Cuiseaux	**26**	C2
Cuisery	**26**	C2
Culan	**30**	B3
Culemborg	**5**	E3
Culoz	**32**	C3
Cusset	**31**	D3
Cuvilly	**11**	E1

D

Dabo	**21**	E3
Dammartin-en-Goële	**18**	C3
Dampierre	**27**	D3
Dampierre-sur-Boutonne	**28**	C3
Dampierre-sur-Salon	**27**	D4
Damville	**17**	F2
Damvillers	**13**	D2
Dangé-St-Romain	**24**	A2
Dannemarie	**21**	E1
Daoulas	**14**	A2
Darney	**20**	C2
Dax	**40**	B3
Deauville	**17**	D3
Decazeville	**36**	B2
Decize	**25**	F2
De Cocksdorp	**2**	C3
Dedemsvaart	**3**	E1
De Haan	**4**	A2
Deinze	**4**	B1
De Koog	**2**	C3
De Kooy	**2**	C2
Delden	**6**	B4
Delft	**4**	C3
Delfzijl	**3**	F3
Delle	**21**	D1
Delme	**20**	C4
Denain	**12**	A4
Den Burg	**2**	C2
Dendermonde	**4**	C1
Denekamp	**6**	C4
Den Haag	**4**	C4
Den Helder	**2**	B2
Den Oever	**2**	C2
De Panne	**4**	A2
Derval	**22**	C3
Descartes	**24**	B2
Desvres	**11**	D3
Deurne	**5**	E2
Deventer	**6**	B4
Die	**32**	B1
Diekirch	**9**	E2
Dieppe	**10**	C2
Dieren	**6**	B3
Diest	**5**	D1
Dieulefit	**38**	B4
Dieulouard	**20**	C3
Dieuze	**21**	D3
Diever	**3**	E2
Differdange	**9**	D1
Digne	**39**	D3
Digoin	**31**	E3
Dijon	**26**	C3
Diksmuide	**4**	A2
Dinan	**15**	E2
Dinant	**8**	C3
Dinard	**15**	E3
Dinoze	**21**	D2
Dissel	**17**	F3
Dives-sur-Mer	**17**	D3
Divonne	**27**	E1
Doesburg	**6**	B3
Doetinchem	**6**	B3
Dokkum	**3**	D3
Dol-de-Bretagne	**15**	E2
Dole	**27**	D3
Dombasle	**20**	C3
Dombrot-le-Sec	**20**	C2
Domburg	**4**	B3
Domèvre-en-Haye	**20**	C3
Domfront	**16**	C2
Domme	**35**	F3
Dompaire	**20**	C2
Dompierre	**31**	E3
Domrémy-la-Pucelle	**20**	B3

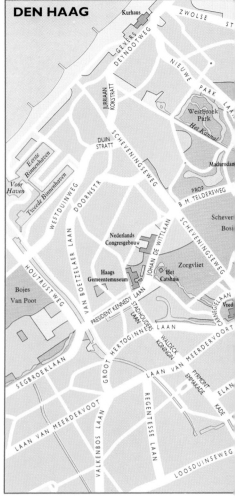

DEN HAAG

Dontilly

Doulevant-le-Château	**20**	A2
Doullens	**11**	E2
Dourdan	**18**	B2
Douvaine	**27**	E1
Douzy	**13**	D3
Dozulé	**17**	D3
Drachten	**3**	D2
Draguignan	**39**	D2
Dreux	**17**	D2
Driebergen	**5**	E3
Dronten	**3**	D1
Drusenheim	**21**	F3
Druten	**5**	E3
Ducey	**16**	B2
Duclair	**17**	E4
Dudelange	**9**	E1
Duingt	**33**	D3
Dun	**13**	D2
Dunkerque	**11**	E4
Dunkerque Ouest	**11**	D4
Dun-le-Palestel	**30**	A3
Dun-sur-Auron	**25**	E2
Duras	**35**	D3
Durban-Corbières	**42**	C2
Durbury	**9**	D3
Durtal	**23**	F3
Dwingeloo	**3**	E2

E

Eaux-Bonnes	**40**	C2
Eaux-Chaudes	**40**	C2
Eauze	**41**	D4
Ebreuil	**31**	D3
Echallon	**32**	C4
Echternach	**9**	E2
Ecommoy	**24**	A4
Ecouis	**18**	A4
Ecueillé	**24**	C2
Ecury	**19**	E3
Edam	**2**	C1
Ede	**5**	E3
Eeklo	**4**	B2
Eelde-Paterswolde	**3**	E3
Eghezée	**8**	C4
Egletons	**30**	B1
Egmond aan Zee	**2**	B2
Eguzon	**30**	A3
Ehnen	**9**	E1
Eibergen	**6**	B3
Eindhoven	**5**	E2
Elbeuf	**17**	E3
Elburg	**3**	D1
Elne	**42**	C1
Elst	**5**	F3
Embrun	**39**	D4
Emmeloord	**3**	D2
Emmen	**3**	E2
Enghien	**8**	B4
Englefontaine	**12**	B4
Enkhuizen	**2**	C2
Enschede	**6**	C4
Ensisheim	**21**	E1
Entraygues-sur-Truyère	**36**	C2
Entrevaux	**39**	E3
Epannes	**28**	C3
Epe	**6**	A4
Épernay	**19**	E3
Épernon	**18**	A3

Dontilly	**18**	C2
Donzenac	**36**	A4
Donzère	**38**	A4
Donzy	**25**	E3
Doorn	**5**	E3
Doornik (Tournai)	**8**	A4
Dordives	**18**	C2
Dordrecht	**5**	D3
Dormans	**12**	B2
Dornes	**25**	F2
Dortan	**27**	D1
Douai	**11**	F3
Douarnenez	**14**	A2
Douchy	**18**	C1
Doucier	**27**	D2
Doudeville	**10**	B1
Doué-la-Fontaine	**23**	F2
Doulaincourt	**20**	B2

Épinal .... **21** D2
Epône .... **18** A3
Erbalunga .... **44** C4
Ermelo .... **5** E4
Ermenonville .... **18** C4
Erneé .... **16** B1
Erquy .... **15** D3
Erstein .... **21** E3
Ervy-le-Châtel .... **19** E1
Esch .... **9** D2
Esch-sur-Alzette .... **9** D1
Espalion .... **36** C2
Espelette .... **40** A3
Estagel .... **42** C1
Estaires .... **11** E3
Esternay .... **19** D3
Estissac .... **19** E2
Estrées-St-Denis .... **18** C4
Étables-sur-Mer .... **15** D3
Etain .... **13** E2
Etalle .... **9** D2
Étampes .... **18** B2
Etaples .... **11** D3
Etretat .... **10** A1
Ettelbruck .... **9** E2
Eu .... **10** C2
Eupen .... **9** E4
Europoort .... **4** C3
Evaux-les-Bains .... **30** C3
Evian .... **27** E1
Evisa .... **44** B3
Evran .... **15** E2
Evreux .... **17** F3
Evron .... **16** C1
Evry .... **18** B3
Excideuil .... **35** F4
Exmes .... **17** D2
Eygvieres .... **38** B2
Eygurande .... **30** C2
Eymet .... **35** E3
Eymoutiers .... **30** A2

Flers .... **16** C2
Fleurance .... **41** E3
Fleuré .... **29** E3
Fleurus .... **8** B3
Fleury .... **17** F3
Flins .... **18** B3
Flize .... **12** C3
Flogny-la-Chapelle .... **19** E1
Florac .... **37** D2
Florennes .... **8** B3
Florenville .... **8** C2
Flumet .... **33** D3
Foix .... **42** A2
Fontainebleau .... **18** C2
Fontaine-Française .... **26** C4
Fontaine-le-Dun .... **10** B2
Fontenay-le-Comte .... **28** C3
Fontenay-Trésigny .... **18** C3
Font-Romeu .... **42** B1
Forbach .... **21** D4
Forcalquier .... **38** C3
Forges-les-Eaux .... **10** C1
Formerie .... **11** D1
Fos .... **41** E1
Fosses .... **8** C3
Fos-sur-Mer .... **38** B2
Foucarmont .... **10** C2
Fouesnant .... **14** B1
Fougères .... **16** B1
Fougerolles .... **21** D1
Foulain .... **20** B2
Fouras .... **28** B2
Fourcès .... **41** D4
Fourmies .... **12** B4
Fournels .... **37** D3
Fours .... **26** A2
Fraize .... **21** D2
Francardo .... **44** B3
Franeker .... **3** D3
Frangy .... **32** C4
Frayssinet .... **36** A2
Fréjus .... **39** E2
Fresnay-sur-Sarthe .... **17** D1
Fresnes .... **11** E3
Fresnes .... **20** C2
Fresnes-en-Woëvre .... **13** E2
Fréteval .... **24** B4
Fretigney .... **27** D4
Frévent .... **11** E3
Freyming Merlebach .... **13** F2
Froissy .... **11** D1
Fromentel .... **16** C2
Fronsac .... **41** E3
Frontignan .... **43** E3
Fruges .... **11** D3
Fumay .... **12** C3
Fumel .... **35** E2
Furnès (Veurne) .... **4** A2

F

Facture .... **34** B3
Falaise .... **17** D3
Fanjeaux .... **42** B2
Farebersviller .... **21** D4
Faucogney .... **21** D1
Faulquemont .... **13** F2
Fauville .... **10** B1
Faverges .... **33** D3
Faverney .... **20** C1
Fayence .... **39** E2
Fayl-Billot .... **20** B1
Fécamp .... **10** B2
Felletin .... **30** B2
Fénétrange .... **21** D4
Fère-Champenoise .... **19** E3
Fère-en-Tardenois .... **12** A2
Ferrette .... **21** E1
Ferrières .... **18** C1
Feurs .... **31** E2
Figari .... **44** B1
Figeac .... **36** B2
Firminy .... **37** E4
Fismes .... **12** B2
Flaine .... **33** D4
Flavigny-sur-Moselle .... **20** C3

G

Gabarret .... **41** D4
Gacé .... **17** D2
Gaël .... **15** E1
Gaillac .... **42** B4
Gaillon .... **17** F3
Gallargues .... **43** E3
Gamaches .... **10** C2
Gan .... **40** C2

Gand (Gent)	4	B1
Ganges	43	E4
Gannat	31	D3
Gap	39	D4
Gardanne	38	C2
Gavarnie	41	D1
Gavray	16	B3
Gedinne	8	C2
Geel	5	D2
Geertruidenberg	5	D3
Geldrop	5	E2
Geleen	5	E1
Gembloux	8	C4
Gémenos	38	C1
Gemert	5	E2
Gémozac	28	C2
Genappe	8	B4
Gençay	29	E3
Génelard	26	B2
Genk	5	E1
Genlis	26	C3
Gennes	23	F3
Gennep	5	F3
Génolhac	37	E2
Gent (Gand)	4	B1
Gentioux	30	B2
Geraardsbergen	4	C1
Gérardmer	21	D2
Gerbéviller	21	D3
Germay	20	B3
Gevrey-Chambertin	26	C3
Gex	27	E1
Ghisonaccia	44	C2
Ghisoni	44	B2
Gien	25	E4
Giens	39	D1
Gieten	3	E2
Giethoorn	3	D2
Gignac	43	D3
Gimont	41	E3
Giromagny	21	D1
Gisors	18	A4
Gistel	4	A2
Givet	12	C4
Givors	32	A3
Givry	26	B2
Givry	8	B3
Givry-en-Argonne	20	A4
Gizeux	24	A3
Glénic	30	B3
Goderville	10	B1
Goes	4	C2
Goirle	5	D2
Golfe Juan	39	E2
Goncelin	32	C2
Gondrecourt	20	B3
Gondrin	41	D4
Goor	6	B4
Gordes	38	B3
Gorinchem	5	D3
Gorredijk	3	D2
Gorron	16	C2
Gosselies	8	B3
Gouarec	14	C2
Gouda	5	D3
Goumois	27	F3
Gourdon	36	A3
Gourin	14	B2
Gournay-en-Bray	11	D1
Gouzon	30	B3
Graçay	24	C2
Gramat	36	A3
Grancey	26	C4
Grandcamp	16	B4
Grand-Champ	22	B4
Grande Fougeray	22	C4
Grandpré	12	C2
Grandrieu	37	E3
Grandvilliers	11	D1
Granges-sur-Vologne	21	D2
Granville	16	B3
Grasse	39	E2
Graulhet	42	B3
Grave	5	E3
Gravelines	11	D4
Gray	27	D4
Grenade	40	C3
Grenade	41	F3
Grenoble	32	C2
Gréoux-les-Bains	38	C2
Grevenmacher	9	E2
Grez-en-Bouère	23	E4
Grignan	38	B4
Grignols	35	D2
Grimaud	39	D1
Grisolles	41	F3
Groenlo	6	B3
Groningen	3	E3
Grostenquin	13	F1
Grouw	3	D2
Gruissan	43	D2
Guebwiller	21	E2
Guémené-Penfao	22	C3
Guer	22	C4
Guérande	22	B3
Guéret	30	B3
Guérigny	25	F2
Guethary	40	A3
Gueugnon	26	A2
Guichen	22	C4
Guignes	18	C3
Guillaumes	39	E3
Guillestre	33	D1
Guilvinec	14	A1
Guînes	11	D4
Guingamp	14	C2
Guipry	22	C4
Guise	12	B3
Guitres	35	D3
Gujan-Mestras	34	B3
Gy	27	D3

H

Haaksbergen	6	C4
Haarlem	2	B1
Habay	9	D2
Hagetmau	40	C3
Hagondange	13	E2
Haguenau	21	F4
Halle	8	B4
Halsteren	4	C2
Ham	11	F1
Hamoir	9	D3
Hannut	8	C4
Hans-sur-Lesse	8	C3
Hardelot-Plage	10	C3
Hardenberg	3	E1
Harderwijk	5	E4
Haren	3	E3
Harfleur	17	D4

Harlingen	2	C3
Haroué	20	C3
Hasparren	40	B3
Hasselt	3	D1
Hasselt	5	D1
Hattem	3	D1
Haut-Asco	44	B3
Hauteville Plage	16	B3
Havelange	8	C3
Hayange	13	E2
Hazebrouck	11	E4
Hechtel	5	E1
Hédé	15	E2
Heemsted	2	B1
Heerde	3	D1
Heerenveen	3	D2
Heerlen	5	F1
Heeze	5	E2
Heino	3	D1
Heist	4	B2
Hellendoorn	3	E1
Hellevoetsluis	4	C3
Helmond	5	E2
Héming	21	D3
Hendaye	40	A3
Hengelo	6	C4
Hénin Beaumont	11	E3
Hennebont	22	A4
Henrichement	25	D3
Herbault	24	B3
Herbestnal	9	E4
Herbeumont	8	C2
Herentals	5	D2
Héricourt	27	E4
Hérisson	30	C3
Herment	30	C2
Herselt	5	D1
Hesdin	11	D3
Hettange	13	E2
Heyrieux	32	B3
Hiersac	29	D2
Hillegom	5	D4
Hilvarenbeek	5	E2
Hilversum	5	E4
Hirsingue	21	E1
Hirson	12	B3
Hochfelden	21	E3
Hoedekenskerre	4	C2
Hoek van Holland	4	C3
Hollum	3	D3
Holten	6	B4
Holwerd	3	D3
Homps	42	C2
Honfleur	17	D4
Hoogerheide	4	C2
Hoogeveen	3	E2
Hoogezand	3	E3
Hoogkarspel	2	C2
Hoogstraten	5	D2
Hoorn	2	C2
Hordain	12	A4
Hornoy	11	D2
Horst	5	F2
Hossegor	40	A3
Hostens	34	C2
Hotton	9	D3
Houdain	11	E3
Houdan	18	A3
Houdelaincourt	20	B3
Houeillès	35	D2
Houffalize	9	D3
Houlgate	17	D3

Hourtin	33	B4
Hourtin Plage	34	B4
Hucqueliers	11	D3
Huelgoat	14	B2
Huizen	2	C2
Hulst	4	C2
Huriel	30	C3
Huy	8	C3
Hyeres	39	D1

I

Ieper (Ypres)	4	A1
Ijmuiden	2	B1
Illiers	17	E1
Imphy	25	F2
Ingelmunster	4	B1
Ingwiller	21	E4
Isdes	25	D4
Isigny	16	B3
Isola	39	E3
Isola 2000	39	E3
Issoire	31	D1
Issoudun	25	D2
Is-sur-Tille	26	C4
Istres	38	B2
Itxassou	40	A3
Ivry-la-Bataille	18	A3
Izegem	4	B1
Izenore	32	C4

J

Jaligny-sur-Besbre	31	D3
Janville	18	B2
Janzé	23	D4
Jard-sur-Mer	28	B3
Jargeau	25	D4
Jarnac	29	D2
Jarnages	30	B3
Jarny	13	E2
Jausiers	39	E4
Javron	16	C2
Jeumont	12	B4
Jodoigne	8	C4
Joigny	19	D1
Joinville	20	B3
Jonzac	28	C1
Josselin	15	D1
Jougne	27	E2
Joure	3	D2
Joyeuse	37	E2
Juan-les-Pins	39	E2
Jugon	15	E2
Juillac	35	F4
Jullouville	16	B2
Jumeaux	31	D1
Jumièges	17	E4
Juniville	12	C2
Jussey	20	C1
Juvigny-le-Tertre	16	B2
Juzennecourt	20	A2

K

Kaatsheuvel	5	D3
Kampen	3	D1
Kasterlee	5	D2
Katwijk aan Zee	4	C4
Kaysersberg	21	E2
Kerkrade	5	F1
Klazienaveen	3	F2
Knokke-Heist	4	B2
Koksijde-Bad	4	A2
Kortrijk (Courtrai)	4	B1
Kotten	6	B3
Krimpen	5	D3
Kruiningen	4	C2

L

La Bassée	11	E3
Labastide-d'Armagnac	41	D4
Labastide-Murat	36	A2
La Bastide-Puylaurent	37	E2
La Bastode de-Sérou	42	A2
La Bâtie-Neuve	39	D4
La Baule	22	B3
La Bazouche-Gouët	17	E1
La Belle Etoile	19	E2
Labenne	40	A3
La Bérarde	33	D1
L'Aber-Wrac'h	14	A3
Labouheyre	34	B2
La Bourboule	30	C1
Labréde	34	C3
La Bresse	21	D2
La Brillane	38	C3
Labrit	34	C1
Lacanau	34	B3
Lacanau-Océan	34	B3
La Canourgue	37	D2
La Capelle	12	B3
Lacapelle-Marival	36	B3
La Capte	39	D1
La Cateau	12	A4
Lacaune	42	C3
La Cavalerie	37	D1
La Celle-Dunoise	30	B3
La Chaise Dieu	37	E4
La Chambre	33	D2
La Chapelle	32	A4
La Chapelle-d'Angillon	25	D3
La Chapelle-en-Vercors	32	B1
La Chapelle-Glain	23	D3
La Charité	25	E2
La Chartre	24	A4
La Châtaigneraie	28	C4
La Châtre	30	B4
La Ciotat	38	C1
La Clayette	31	F3
La Clusaz	33	D3
La Cluse	32	C4
La Cluse-et-Mijoux	27	E2
La Coquille	29	F1
La Côte-St-Andre	32	B2
La Courtine	30	B2
Lacq	40	C3
La Croisère	30	A3
La Croixille	16	B1
La Croix-Valmer	39	E1
La Cure	27	E1
Ladon	18	C1
La Fère	12	A3
Laferté	20	B1
La Ferté-Bernard	17	E1
La Ferté Gaucher	19	D3
La Ferté Macé	16	C2
La Ferté-Milon	18	C4
La Ferté-sous-Jouarre	18	C3
La Ferté-St-Aubin	25	D4
La Ferté-Vidame	17	E2
Laffrey	32	C2
La Flèche	23	F3
La Flotte	28	B3
Lafrançaise	35	F1
La Gacilly	22	C4
La Garde-Freinet	39	D1
Lagniueu	32	B3
Lagny	18	C3
La Grand-Combe	37	E1
La Grande-Motte	43	E3
Lagrasse	42	C2
La Grave	33	D2
Laguepie	36	B1
La Guerche	25	E2
La Guerche-de-Bretagne	23	D4
Laguiole	36	C2
La Haye-du-Puits	16	B3
La Hutte	17	D1
L'Aigle	17	E2
Laignes	19	E1
L'Aiguillon	28	B3
Laissac	36	C2
La Javie	39	D3
Lalinde	35	E3
La Loupe	17	E2
Lalouvesc	37	F3
La Louvière	8	B3
L'Alpe-d'Huez	32	C2
La Machine	25	F2
La Malène	37	D2
Lamalou-les-Bains	43	D3
Lamarche	20	C2
Lamarque	34	C3
Lamastre	32	A1
La Maucarrière	23	F1
Lamballe	15	D2
Lambesc	38	B2
La Mongie	41	D2
La Mothe-Achard	28	A4
Lamotte-Beuvron	25	D3
La Motte-Chalancon	38	B4
Lampaul-Plourzel	14	A2
La Mure	32	C1
Lamure	31	F2
La Napoule-Plage	39	E2
Landerneau	14	B2
Landévennec	14	A2
Landivisiau	14	B2
Landivy	16	B2
Landrecies	12	B4
La Neuve-Lyre	17	E3
Langeac	37	D3
Langeais	24	A3
Langentière	37	F2
Langogne	37	E3
Langoiran	34	C3
Langon	35	D2
Langres	20	B1

Lanmeur	**14**	B3	Le Barp	**34**	C2
Lannemezan	**41**	D2	Le Beausset	**38**	C1
Lannilis	**14**	A3	Le Blanc	**24**	B1
Lannion	**14**	C3	Le Boulou	**42**	C1
Lanouaille	**29**	F1	Le Bourg d'Oisans	**32**	C2
Lanslebourg	**33**	E2	Le Bourget	**32**	C3
Lantosque	**39**	F3	Le Bugue	**35**	E3
Lanvollon	**14**	C3	Le Cap d'Agde	**43**	D2
Laon	**12**	B3	Le Cateau	**12**	A4
La Pacaudière	**31**	E3	Le Catelet	**12**	A3
Lapalisse	**31**	D3	Le Caylar	**43**	D4
La Pallice	**28**	B3	L'Echalp	**33**	E1
La Palmyre	**28**	B2	Le Chateau-d'Oléron	**28**	B2
La Palud-sur-Verdon	**39**	D2	Le Châtelard	**33**	D3
La Petite-Pierre	**21**	E4	Le Châtelet	**30**	B4
La Plagne	**33**	D3	Le Chesne	**12**	C2
Laplume	**35**	E1	Le Cheylard	**37**	F3
Lapoutroie	**21**	E2	Le Conquet	**14**	A2
Laragne-Montéglin	**38**	C3	Le Creusot	**26**	B2
L'Arbresle	**32**	A3	Le Croisic	**22**	B3
Larche	**36**	A3	Le Crotoy	**11**	D2
Larche	**39**	E4	Lectoure	**41**	E4
La Réole	**35**	D2	Lédignan	**43**	E4
L'Argentiere-la-Bessée	**33**	D1	Le Donjon	**31**	E3
Larmor	**22**	A4	Le Dorat	**29**	F3
La Roche-Bernard	**22**	B3	Leek	**3**	E3
La Roche-Chalais	**35**	D4	Leerdam	**5**	D3
La Roche-en-Ardenne	**9**	D3	Leeuwarden	**3**	D3
La Rochefoucauld	**29**	E2	Le Faou	**14**	B2
La Rochelle	**28**	B3	Le Faouët	**14**	C1
La Roche-Posay	**24**	B2	Le Fossat	**42**	A2
La-Roches-sur-Foron	**33**	D4	Legé	**22**	C2
La Roche-sur-Yon	**23**	D1	Le Grand Bourg	**30**	A3
La Rochette	**33**	D2	Le Grand-Lucé	**24**	A4
Larochette	**9**	E2	Le Grand-Pressigny	**24**	B2
Laroquebrou	**36**	B3	Le Grau-du-Roi	**43**	E3
La Roquebrussanne	**39**	D1	Léguevin	**41**	F3
Laroque-des-Arcs	**36**	A2	Le Havre	**17**	D4
La Roque-Gageac	**35**	F3	Le Hohwald	**21**	E3
Larrau	**40**	B2	Leiden	**5**	D4
Laruns	**40**	C2	Le Lauzet-Ubaye	**39**	D4
La Salvetat	**36**	B2	Le Lavandou	**39**	D1
La Salvetat-sur-Agout	**42**	C3	Le Lion-D'Angers	**23**	E3
La Seyne	**38**	C1	Le Logis-du-Pin	**39**	E2
La Souterraine	**30**	A3	Le Loroux Bottereau	**23**	D2
Lassay	**16**	C2	Le Louroux	**23**	E3
Lassigny	**11**	E1	Le Luc	**39**	D2
La Suze	**23**	F4	Le Lude	**24**	A4
Latour de Carol	**42**	B1	Lelystad	**2**	C1
La Tour-du-Pin	**32**	B3	Le Mans	**24**	A4
La Tranche-sur-Mer	**28**	B3	Le Markstein	**21**	D2
La Tremblade	**28**	B2	Le Mas-d'Azil	**41**	F2
La Trimouille	**29**	F3	Le Mayet	**31**	E3
La Trinité	**22**	A3	Lembach	**21**	E4
La Trinité-Porhoët	**15**	D1	Lembeye	**41**	D3
La Turbie	**39**	F2	Le Merlerault	**17**	D2
Laubrières	**23**	D4	Lemmer	**3**	D2
Laurière	**30**	A2	Le Monastier	**37**	E3
Lauterbourg	**21**	F4	Le Monêtier	**33**	D1
Lautrec	**42**	B3	Le Mont-Dore	**30**	C1
Lauwersoog	**3**	E3	Le Montet	**31**	D3
Lauzerte	**35**	F2	Le Mont-St Michel	**16**	B2
Lauzun	**35**	E2	Lempdes	**31**	D2
Laval	**23**	E4	Le Muret	**34**	C2
Lavardac	**35**	D1	Le Muy	**39**	D1
Lavaur	**42**	B3	Lencloître	**24**	A2
Lavelanet	**42**	B2	Le Neubourg	**17**	E3
La Voulte	**32**	A1	Le Nouvion-en-Thierache	**12**	B4
Lavoûte-Chilhac	**37**	D3	Lens	**11**	E3
Lavoûte-sur-Loire	**37**	E3	Léon	**40**	B4
La Wantzenau	**21**	F3	Leopoldsburg	**5**	E1
Le Bar	**39**	E2	Le Palais	**22**	A3

Le Péage-de-Rousillon	32	A2
Le Perthus	42	C1
Le Pin-au-Haras	17	D2
Le Pont-de-Beauvoision	32	C3
Le Pont-de-Claix	32	C2
Le Pontet d'Eyrans	34	C4
Le Portel	10	C3
Le Pouldu	22	A4
Le Pouré-sur-Vie	23	D1
Le Pouzin	32	A1
Le Puy	37	E3
Le Quesnoy	12	B4
Le Rabot	25	D4
Le Rozier	37	D1
Le Russey	27	E3
Les Abrets	32	C3
Les Adrets	39	E2
Les Aix	25	E3
Les Andelys	18	A4
Les Arcs	33	E3
Les Arcs	39	D2
Les Baux	38	B2
Les Cabannes	42	A1
Lescar	40	C2
L'Escarène	39	F3
Les Contamines	33	D3
Les Deux-Alpes	33	D2
Les Echarmeaux	31	F3
Les Echelles	32	C2
Les Epesses	23	E2
Les Essarts	23	D1
Les Eyzies	35	F3
Les Gets	33	D4
Les Halles	31	F2
Les Hayons	10	C1
Les Herbiers	23	D2
Les Houches	33	E3
Les Issambres	39	E2
Les Laumes	26	B4
Les Lecques	38	C1
Les Menuires	33	D2
Lesneven	14	A3
Lesparre-Médoc	34	B4
Les Pieux	16	A4
Les Planches	27	D2
Les Ponts-de Ce	23	E3
Les Riceys	19	E1
Les Rosiers	23	F3
Les Rousses	27	E2
Les Sables-d'Olonne	28	A4
Lessay	16	B3
Lessines	8	A4
Lestelle Bétharram	40	C2
Les Trois-Epis	21	E2
Les Trois-Moutiers	23	F2
Les Vans	37	E2
Les Verrières	27	E2
Le Teil	38	A4
Le Teilleul	16	C2
Le Thillot	21	D1
Le Touquet	10	C3
Le Touvet	32	C2
Le Trayas	39	E2
Le Tréport	10	C2
Leucate	43	D2
Leuglay	20	A1
Leuven (Louvain)	5	D1
Leuze	8	A4
Le Val-André	15	D2
Le Vaudreuil	17	F3
Levens	39	F3
Le Vernet	39	D3
Levet	25	D2
Levie	44	B1
Levier	27	E3
Le Vigan	43	D4
Levroux	24	C2
Lezay	29	D3
Lézignan-Corbières	42	C2
Lezoux	31	D2
Libourne	35	D3
Libramont	9	D2
Lichtenvoorde	6	B3
Liege (Luik)	9	D4
Lier	5	D2
Liernais	26	B3
Lieurey	17	E3
Liffré	16	A1
Ligeuville	9	E3
Lignières	25	D2
Ligny-en-Barrois	20	B3
Ligueil	24	B2
L'Ile Rousse	44	B3
Lille	11	F3
Lillebonne	17	E4
Lillers	11	E3
Limoges	29	F2
Limogne	36	A2
Limonest	32	A3
Limours	18	B3
Limoux	42	B2
Lisieux	17	D3
Lisle	42	B4
L'Isle-Adam	18	B4
L'Isle-de-Noé	41	E3
L'Isle-en-Dodon	41	E2
L'Isle-Jourdain	29	E3
L'Isle-Jourdain	41	F3
L'Isle-sur-la-Sorgue	38	B3
L'Isle-sur-le-Doubs	27	E4
Lisse	5	D4
Lit-en-Mixe	34	B1
Livarot	17	D3
Livernon	36	B2
Livron	32	A1
Lizy	18	C3
L'Ile-Bouchard	24	A3
Lochem	6	B4
Loches	24	B2
Locmaria	22	A3
Locmariaquer	22	A3
Locminé	22	B4
Locquirec	14	B3
Locronan	14	B2
Loctudy	14	B1
Lodève	43	D3
Lohéac	22	C4
Lokeren	4	C2
Lombez	41	E3
Lomme	11	F3
Lommel	5	C2
Londinières	10	C2
Longeau	20	B1
Longny	17	C2
Longué	23	F3
Longuyon	13	E2
Longwy	13	E2
Lons-le-Saunier	27	D2
Lorcé	9	D3
Lorentzen	21	E4
Lorgues	39	D2
Lorient	22	A4
Loriol-sur-Drôme	32	A1
Lormes	26	A3

Lormont	34	C3
Lorris	25	D4
Loudéac	15	D2
Loudes	37	E3
Loudun	23	F3
Louhans	26	C2
Loulay	28	C3
Lourdes	41	D2
Louvain (Leuven)	5	D1
Louviers	17	F3
Luhersac	30	A1
Lucenay	26	B3
Luc-en-Diois	38	C4
Luçon	28	B3
Luc-sur-Mer	16	C3
Luigny	17	E1
Luik (Liege)	9	D4
Lumbres	11	D3
Lummen	5	E1
Lunas	43	D5
Lunel	43	E3
Lunéville	21	D3
Lurcy-Lévis	25	E2
Lure	21	D1
Lureuil	24	B2
Luri	44	C4
Lusignan	29	D3
Lusigny	19	E2
Lus-la-Croix-Haute	38	C4
Lussac-les-Châteaux	29	E3
Lussan	37	F1
Luxembourg	9	E1
Luz-St-Sauveur	41	D1
Luzy	26	A2
Lyon	32	A3
Lyons-la-Forêt	18	A4

M

Maaseik	5	E1
Maasmechelen	5	E1
Maassluis	4	C3
Maastricht	5	E1
Machault	12	C2
Machecoul	22	C2
Mâcon	26	C1
Made	5	D3
Magescq	40	B3
Magnac-Laval	29	F3
Magny-en-Vexin	18	A4
Maîche	27	F3
Mailly-le-Camp	19	E3
Maintenon	18	A2
Malaucène	38	B3
Malbuisson	27	E2
Maldegem	4	B2
Malesherbes	18	B2
Malestroit	22	B4
Malicorne	23	F4
Malines (Mechelen)	5	D1
Malmédy	9	E3
Malo-les-Bains	11	E4
Mamers	17	D1
Mandelieu	39	E2
Manosque	38	C2
Mansle	29	D2
Mantes	18	A3
Manzat	30	C2
Marans	28	B3
Marboz	26	C1
Marchaux	27	E3
Marche-en-Famenne	9	D3
Marcheprime	34	C3
Marciac	41	D3
Marcigny	31	E3
Marcillac-Vallon	36	C2
Marcillat	30	C3
Marcilly-le-Hayer	19	D2
Marckolsheim	21	E2
Marennes	28	B2
Mareuil	28	B4
Mareuil	29	E1
Marignane	38	B2
Marigny-le-Châtel	19	D2
Marines	18	B4
Maringues	31	D2
Marle	12	B3

LILLE

Marlenheim

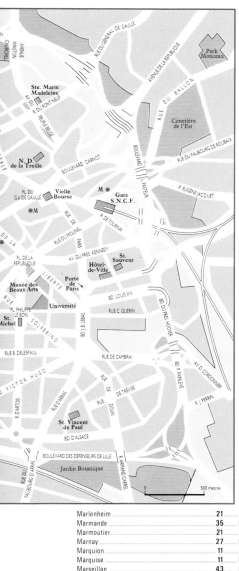

Massey	25	D2
Massiac	37	D4
Matha	29	D2
Mathay	27	F4
Matignon	15	E2
Matour	31	F3
Maubeuge	12	B4
Maubourguet	41	D3
Mauléon	23	E2
Mauléon-Licharre	40	B2
Maulévrier	23	E2
Maupertus	16	B4
Maure	22	C4
Mauriac	36	B4
Mauron	15	D1
Maurs	36	B3
Maury	42	C1
Mauvezin	41	E3
Mauze	28	C3
Mayenne	16	C1
Mayet	24	A4
Mazamet	42	B3
Mazères	42	A2
Meaux	18	C3
Mechelen (Malines)	5	D1
Medemblik	2	C2
Megève	33	D3
Mehun	25	D2
Meijel	5	F2
Mélisey	21	D1
Melle	29	D3
Melun	18	C2
Menan	4	A1
Menat	30	C3
Mende	37	D2
Mens	32	C1
Menthon	33	D3
Menton	39	F2
Meppel	3	D2
Mer	24	C4
Merdrignac	15	D2
Meribel	33	D2
Méréville	18	B2
Meribal	33	D2
Mersch	9	E2
Meru	18	B4
Mervans	26	C2
Méry	19	E2
Meschers-sur-Gironde	28	B2
Meslay	23	E4
Mesnil-Val	10	C2
Mesvres	26	B2
Metabief	27	E2
Méteren	11	E4
Mettet	8	C3
Metz	13	E2
Metzervisse	13	F2
Meulan	18	B3
Meung	24	C4
Meximieux	32	B3
Meymac	30	B1
Meyrargues	38	C2
Meyrueis	37	D1
Meyzieu	32	B3
Mèze	43	E3
Mézel	39	D3
Mézières	29	E3
Mézières-en-Brenne	24	B2
Mézilhac	37	F3
Mézin	35	D1
Middelkerke-Bad	4	A2
Middleburg	4	B2

Marlenheim	21	E3
Marmande	35	D2
Marmoutier	21	E3
Marnay	27	D3
Marquion	11	F2
Marquise	11	D4
Marseillan	43	D3
Marseillan-Plage	43	D2
Marseille	38	C1
Marseille-en-Beauvaisis	11	D1
Martel	36	A3
Martelange	9	D2
Martigné-Ferchard	23	D4
Martigues	38	B2
Marvejols	37	D2
Masevaux	21	D1
Massat	41	F1
Masseube	41	E3

Middleharnis	4	C3
Midsland	2	C3
Miélan	41	D3
Migennes	19	D1
Mijoux	27	D1
Millas	42	C1
Millau	37	D1
Milly	18	B2
Mimizan	34	B2
Mimizan-Plage	34	B2
Mindin	22	C3
Miramar	39	E2
Miramas	38	B2
Mirambeau	28	C1
Miramont-de-Guyenne	35	D2
Mirande	41	D3
Mirebeau	24	A2
Mirebeau	26	C3
Mirecourt	20	C2
Mirepoix	42	B2
Modane	33	D2
Modave	9	D3
Moirans	32	C2
Moirans-en-Montagne	27	D1
Moissac	35	F1
Mol	5	D2
Molières	35	F1
Moloy	26	C4
Molsheim	21	E3
Moncontour	15	D2
Mondorf-les-Bains	9	E1
Monestier-de-Clermont	32	C1
Monflanquin	35	E2
Monistrol-d'Allier	37	E3
Monistrol-sur-Loire	37	E4
Monnickendam	2	C1
Monpazier	35	E3
Monplaisir	24	B4
Mons (Bergen)	8	B3
Monségur	35	D2
Montagnac	43	D3
Montaigu	23	D2
Montaigu-de-Quercy	35	F2
Montaigut	30	C3
Montalivet	28	B1
Montaren	37	F1
Montargis	18	C1
Montastruc-la-Conseillère	42	A3
Montauban	41	F4
Montbard	26	B4
Montbazens	36	B2
Montbazon	24	B3
Montbéliard	27	F4
Montbenoît	27	E3
Montbonnot	32	C2
Montbrison	31	E1
Montbron	29	E2
Montbrun-les-Bains	38	C3
Montceau-les-Mines	26	B2
Montcornet	12	B3
Montcoutant	23	E1
Montcuq	35	F2
Mont-de-Marsan	40	C4
Montdidier	11	E1
Montdoubleau	24	B4
Montebourg	16	B4
Monte-Carlo	39	F2
Montélimar	38	A4
Montendre	34	C4
Montereau	18	C2
Montesquieu-Volvestre	41	F2
Montesquiou	41	D3

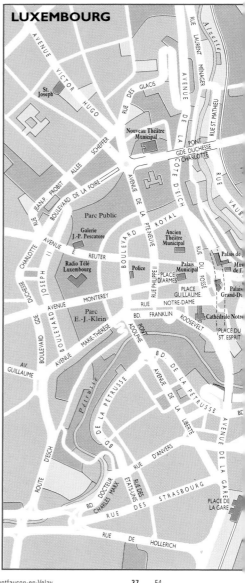

LUXEMBOURG

Montfaucon-en-Velay	37	F4
Montfort	15	E1
Montfort	18	A3
Montfort	40	B3
Montgenèvre	33	E1
Montgiscard	42	A3
Montguyon	35	D4
Montherme	12	C3
Monthois	12	C2
Monthureaux	20	C2

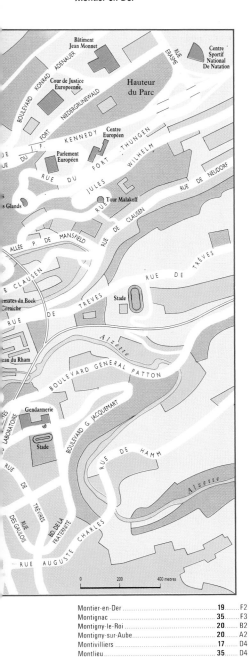

Montmédy	13	D3
Montmélian	32	C3
Montmirail	17	E1
Montmirail	19	D3
Montmirey	27	D3
Montmoreau	29	D1
Montmorillon	29	E3
Montmort	19	D3
Montoire	24	B4
Montpellier	43	E3
Montpezat	36	A2
Montpon-Ménestérol	35	D3
Montpont	26	C2
Montréal	42	B2
Montréal	41	D4
Montréjeau	41	E2
Montrésor	24	B2
Montret	26	C2
Montreuil	11	D3
Montreuil-aux-Lions	19	D3
Montreuil-Bellay	23	F2
Montrevel	26	C1
Montrichard	24	B3
Montrod-les-Bains	31	E2
Montsalvy	36	C3
Montsauche	26	A3
Montsoreau	23	F2
Mont-sous-Vaudrey	27	D3
Monts-sur-Guesnes	24	A2
Montsûrs	16	C1
Morcenx	34	B1
Mordelles	15	E1
Morestel	32	B3
Moreuil	11	E1
Morez	27	D2
Morgat	14	A2
Morhange	21	D4
Morlaàs	40	C2
Morlaix	14	B3
Mormant	18	C2
Morosaglia	44	C3
Mortagne-au-Perche	17	E2
Mortagne-sur-Sèvre	23	D2
Mortain	16	B2
Morteau	27	E3
Mortrée	17	D2
Morzine	33	D4
Mouchard	27	D3
Mougins	39	E2
Mouliherne	23	F3
Moulins	31	D4
Moulins-Engilbert	26	A3
Moulins-la-Marche	17	E2
Moustiers-ste-Marie	39	D3
Mouthe	27	E2
Mouthier	27	E3
Mouthoumet	42	C2
Moutiers	33	D3
Moutiers	28	B4
Mouy	18	B4
Mouzon	13	D3
Mugron	40	C3
Mulhouse	21	E1
Munster	21	E2
Murat	36	C3
Murato	44	C3
Murat-sur-Vebre	42	C3
Mur-de-Barrez	36	C3
Mur-de-Bretagne	14	C2
Muret	41	F3
Muro	44	B3
Musselkanaal	3	F2
Montier-en-Der	19	F2
Montignac	35	F3
Montigny-le-Roi	20	B2
Montigny-sur-Aube	20	A2
Montivilliers	17	D4
Montlieu	35	D4
Mont-Louis	42	B1
Montluçon	30	C3
Montluel	32	B3
Montmarault	30	C3

Mussidan

Mussidan	**35**	E3
Mussy	**19**	F1
Muzillac	**22**	B3

N

Naarden	**5**	E4
Nadrin	**9**	D3
Nailloux	**42**	A3
Najac	**36**	B2
Nalzen	**42**	A2
Namur	**8**	C3
Nancy	**20**	C3
Nangis	**18**	C2
Nans-les-Pins	**38**	C2
Nant	**37**	D1
Nantes	**23**	D2
Nanteuil-le-Haudouin	**18**	C4
Nantiat	**29**	F2
Nantua	**32**	C4
Narbonne	**42**	C2
Narbonne-Plage	**43**	D2
Nasbinals	**37**	D2
Navarrenx	**40**	C2
Navilly	**26**	C2
Neede	**6**	B3
Nemours	**18**	C2
Nérac	**35**	D1
Néris-les-Bains	**30**	C3
Nérondes	**25**	E2
Nes	**3**	D3
Nesle	**11**	E1
Nettancourt	**20**	A3
Neuf-Brisach	**21**	E2
Neufchâteau	**20**	B2
Neufchâteau	**9**	D2
Neufchâtel	**12**	B2
Neufchâtel-en-Bray	**10**	C1
Neuillé Pont-Pierre	**24**	A3
Neuilly-l'Evêque	**20**	B1
Neuilly-St-Front	**12**	A2
Neu Moresnet	**9**	E4
Neung	**24**	C3
Neuves-Maisons	**20**	C3
Neuvic	**35**	E3
Neuvic	**36**	B4
Neuville	**24**	A2
Neuville	**32**	A3
Neuville-aux-Bois	**18**	B1
Neuvy	**30**	B4
Neuvy-sur-Barangeon	**25**	D3
Nevers	**25**	E2
Nexon	**29**	F2
Nice	**39**	F2
Niederbronn	**21**	E4
Nieppe	**11**	E3
Nieuil	**29**	E2
Nieuweschans	**3**	F3
Nieuwpoort	**4**	A2
Nijkerk	**5**	E4
Nijmegen	**5**	F3
Nijverdal	**6**	B4
Nîmes	**43**	F4
Ninove	**4**	C1
Niort	**28**	C3
Nitry	**26**	A4
Nivelles	**8**	B4

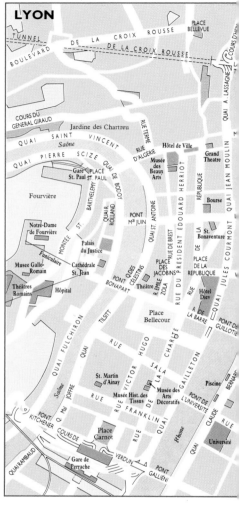

Noailles	**18**	B4
Nœux	**11**	E3
Nogaro	**41**	D3
Nogent	**20**	B2
Nogent-le-Roi	**18**	A3
Nogent-le-Rotrou	**17**	E1
Nogent-sur-Seine	**19**	D2
Noirétable	**31**	E2
Noirmoutier	**22**	B2
Nolay	**26**	B2
Nomeny	**20**	C4
Nomexy	**20**	C2
Nonancourt	**17**	F2
Nonant-le-Pin	**17**	D2
Nontron	**29**	E1
Nonza	**44**	C4
Noordwijk aan Zee	**5**	D4

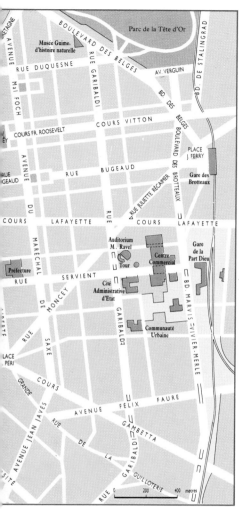

O

Obernai	21	E3
Oirschot	5	E2
Oisement	11	D2
Oisterwijk	5	E2
Olargues	42	C3
Oldenzaal	6	C4
Oletta	44	C3
Olette	42	B1
Olivet	24	C4
Olliergues	31	E2
Olmeto	44	B1
Olonzac	42	C2
Oloron-Ste-Marie	40	C2
Olst	6	B4
Ommen	3	E1
Onnaing	12	A4
Oostburg	4	B2
Oostehout	5	D3
Oostende	4	A2
Oosterbeek	5	F3
Oostérend	2	C3
Oosterwolde	3	E2
Oostmalle	5	D2
Ootmarsum	3	E1
Oraison	38	C3
Orange	38	B3
Orbec	17	E3
Orbey	21	E2
Orchies	12	A4
Orcières	33	D1
Orgelet	27	D2
Orgeval	18	B3
Orgon	38	B2
Orléans	18	B1
Orly	18	B3
Ornans	27	E3
Orthez	40	C3
Oss	5	E3
Otterlo	5	F4
Oucques	24	C4
Oud Beijerland	4	C3
Ouddorp	4	C3
Oudenaarde	4	B1
Oude-Pekela	3	F2
Ouistreham	17	D3
Oust	41	F1
Ouzouer-le-Marche	18	A1
Oyonnax	27	D1

P

Pacy-sur-Eure	17	F3
Pagny	13	E1
Paimbœuf	22	C3
Paimpol	14	C3
Paladru	32	C2
Palavas	43	E3
Paliseul	8	C2
Pamiers	42	A2
Panassac	41	E3
Paray-le-Monial	31	E3
Parentis-en-Born	34	B2
Paris	18	B3

Nordausques	11	D4
Norg	3	E2
Nort	23	D3
Nouan-le-Fuzelier	25	D3
Nouans-les-Fontaines	24	C2
Nouvion	11	D2
Noves	38	B3
Novion-Porcien	12	C3
Noyant	23	F3
Noyers	26	A4
Noyers-sur-Jabron	38	C3
Noyon	11	F1
Nozay	22	C3
Nozeroy	27	D2
Nuits-St-Georges	26	C3
Nunspeet	3	D1
Nyons	38	B4

Parthenay	**29**	D4
Partinello	**44**	B3
Pas de la Casa	**42**	A1
Pas-en-Artois	**11**	E2
Patay	**18**	A1
Pau	**40**	C2
Pauillac	**34**	C4
Paulhaguet	**37**	D4
Pavilly	**10**	B1
Payrac	**36**	A3
Péaule	**22**	B3
Peira-Cava	**39**	F3
Pellegrue	**35**	D3
Pentrez-Plage	**14**	A2
Percy	**16**	B3
Périers	**16**	B3
Périgueux	**35**	E4
Perkpolder	**4**	C2
Pernes	**38**	B3
Péronne	**11**	E2
Pérouges	**32**	B3
Perpignan	**42**	C1
Perros-Guirec	**14**	C3
Pertuis	**38**	C2
Péruwelz	**8**	A4
Pesmes	**27**	D3
Petange	**9**	D1
Petreto-Bicchisano	**44**	B2
Peyrat-le-Château	**30**	B2
Peyrehorade	**40**	B3
Peyrolles	**38**	C2
Peyruis	**38**	C3
Pézenas	**43**	D3
Phalsbourg	**21**	E3
Philippeville	**8**	B3
Piana	**44**	A3
Picquigny	**11**	D2
Piedicroce	**44**	C3
Pierre-Buffiere	**30**	A2
Pierre-de-Bresse	**26**	C2
Pierrefitte	**20**	B4
Pierrefitte-Nestalos	**41**	D2
Pierrefonds	**18**	C4
Pierrefort	**36**	C3
Pierrelatte	**38**	A4
Pierroton	**34**	C3
Pilat-Plage	**34**	B2
Piney	**19**	E2
Pino	**44**	C4
Pinols	**37**	D3
Pionsat	**30**	C3
Pipriac	**22**	C4
Piriac	**22**	B3
Pirou-Plage	**16**	B3
Pissos	**34**	C2
Pithiviers	**18**	B2
Plabennec	**14**	A2
Plaisance	**41**	D3
Plancoët	**15**	E2
Pleaux	**36**	B3
Plélan-le-Grand	**15**	E1
Plestin	**14**	C3
Pleumartin	**24**	B2
Pleyben	**14**	B2
Ploërmel	**15**	D1
Plombières	**21**	D2
Plonéour Lanvern	**14**	A1
Plouaret	**14**	B3
Plouay	**14**	C1
Ploubalay	**15**	E2
Ploudalmezeau	**14**	A3
Plouescat	**14**	B3

MARSEILLE

Plougasnou	**14**	B3
Plouguenast	**15**	D2
Plouha	**15**	D3
Plouigneau	**14**	B3
Plouray	**14**	C2
Plozévet	**14**	A1
Pluvigner	**22**	A4
Podensac	**34**	C3
Poeldijk	**4**	C3
Pointe de Grave	**28**	B2

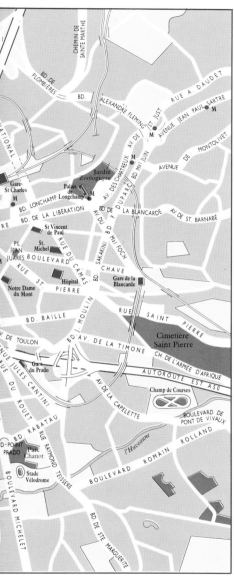

Pontacq	41	D2
Pontailler	26	C3
Pont-à-Mousson	20	C4
Pontarion	30	B2
Pontarlier	27	E2
Pontaubault	16	B2
Pont-Audemer	17	E3
Pontaumur	30	C2
Pont-Aven	14	B1
Pontcharra	32	C2
Pontchartrain	18	B3
Pontchâteau	22	C3
Pont-Croix	14	A1
Pont-d'Ain	32	B4
Pont-de-Briques	10	C3
Pont-de-Dore	31	D2
Pont-de-l'Arche	17	F3
Pont-de-Roide	27	F3
Pont de Salars	36	C2
Pont-de-Vaux	26	C1
Ponte-Leccia	44	B3
Pont-en-Royans	32	B2
Pontgibaud	30	C2
Pontigny	19	D1
Pontivy	14	C1
Pont-l'Abbe	14	A1
Pont-l'Évêque	17	D3
Pontlevoy	24	B3
Pontoise	18	B3
Pont-Réan	22	C4
Pontrieux	14	C3
Pont Scorff	22	A4
Pont-St-Esprit	38	A3
Pont-St-Vincent	20	C3
Pont-sur-Yonne	19	D2
Pontvallain	24	A4
Poperinge	4	A1
Pornic	22	C2
Pornichet	22	B3
Porquerolles	39	D1
Portbail	16	A4
Port-Barcarès	43	D1
Port Camargue	43	E3
Port-Cros	39	D1
Port-de-Bouc	38	B2
Port-en-Bessin	16	C4
Port Grimaud	39	E1
Porticcio	44	B2
Port-la-Nouvelle	43	D2
Port-Leucate	43	D2
Port-Louis	22	A4
Port-Manech	14	B1
Port-Navalo	22	A3
Porto	44	B3
Portorson	16	B2
Porto-Vecchio	44	C1
Port-Ste Marie	35	E2
Port-St-Louis-du-Rhône	38	B2
Port-sur-Saône	20	C1
Port-Vendres	43	D1
Pouancé	23	D3
Pougues-les-Eaux	25	E2
Pouilly	25	E3
Pouilly-en-Auxois	26	B3
Pouyastruc	41	D2
Pouzauges	23	E2
Pradelles	37	E3
Prades	42	C1
Prahecq	29	D3
Pralognan	33	E2
Prats-de-Mollo	42	C1
Prauthoy	26	C4

Pointe de Penmarch	14	A1
Pointe du Raz	14	A1
Poissons	20	B3
Poitiers	29	E4
Poix	11	D2
Poix-Terron	12	C3
Poligny	27	D2
Pompey	20	C3
Poncin	32	B4
Pons	28	C2

Précy-sous-Thil .... **26** B3
Pré-en-Pail .... **17** D2
Prémery .... **25** F2
Pressac .... **29** E3
Preuilly-sur-Claise .... **24** B2
Primel-Trégastel .... **14** B3
Privas .... **32** A1
Profondeville .... **8** C3
Propriano .... **44** B1
Provins .... **19** D2
Prunete-Cervione .... **44** C3
Puget-sur-Argens .... **39** E2
Puget-Théniers .... **39** E3
Puget-Ville .... **39** D1
Puiseaux .... **18** B2
Puivert .... **42** B2
Purmerend .... **2** C1
Putanges .... **16** C2
Puttelange .... **21** D4
Putten .... **5** E4
Puy de Dôme .... **30** C2
Puy-Guillaume .... **31** D2
Puylaurens .... **42** B3
Puy-l'Evêque .... **35** F2
Pyla-sur-Mer .... **34** B3

Q

Quarré-le-Tombes .... **26** A3
Questembert .... **22** B3
Quettehou .... **16** B4
Quiberon .... **22** A3
Quillan .... **42** B2
Quimper .... **14** B1
Quimperle .... **14** B1
Quinéville .... **16** B4
Quingey .... **27** D3
Quintin .... **15** D2
Quissac .... **43** E4

R

Raalte .... **6** B4
Rabastens .... **42** A4
Rabastens-de-Bigorre .... **41** D3
Rambervillers .... **21** D2
Rambouillet .... **18** A3
Randan .... **31** D2
Rânes .... **17** D2
Raon-l'Etape .... **21** D3
Raversijde .... **4** A2
Rayol .... **39** D1
Réalmont .... **42** B3
Rebais .... **19** D3
Recey-sur-Ource .... **20** A1
Recologne .... **27** D3
Redon .... **22** C3
Reignier .... **33** D4
Reims .... **12** B2
Rémalard .... **17** E1
Remich .... **9** E1
Remiremont .... **21** D2
Remouchamps .... **9** D3
Remoulins .... **38** A3
Rémuzat .... **38** B4
Renaison .... **31** E2
Renaix (Ronse) .... **4** B1

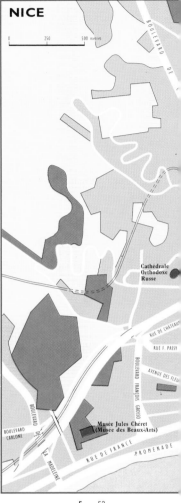

NICE

0 .... 250 .... 500 metres

Cathédrale
Orthodoxe
Russe

Musée Jules Chéret
(Musée des Beaux-Arts)

Renkum .... **5** E3
Rennes .... **15** E1
Réquista .... **36** C1
Ressons .... **11** E1
Rethel .... **12** C2
Retiers .... **23** D4
Retournac .... **37** E4
Reuilly .... **25** D2
Reusel .... **5** D2
Revel .... **42** B3
Révigny .... **20** A3
Revin .... **12** C3
Rhenen .... **5** E3
Rhinau .... **21** E2
Riaillé .... **23** D3
Rians .... **38** C2
Ribeauville .... **21** E2
Ribécourt .... **11** E1

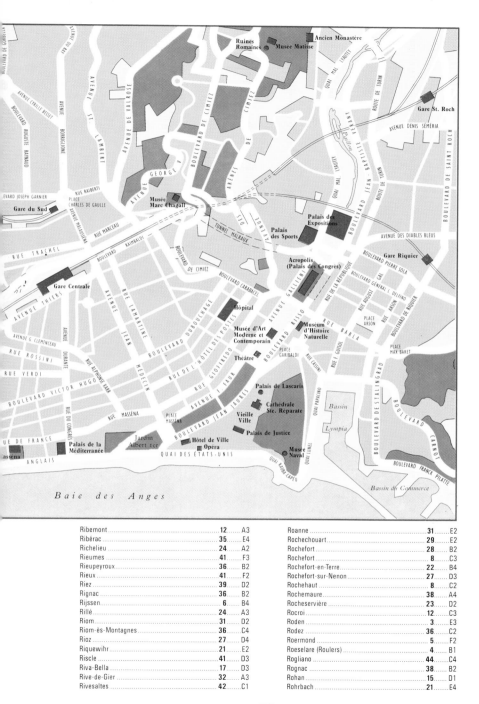

Roisel	11	F2
Romans-sur-Isère	32	B2
Rombas	13	E2
Romilly-sur-Seine	19	D2
Romorantin-Lanthenay	24	C3
Ronchamp	21	D1
Ronse (Renaix)	4	B1
Roodeschool	3	E3
Roosendaal	5	D2
Roquebilliere	39	F3
Roquebrune-Cap-Martin	39	F2
Roquefort	34	C1
Roquefort-sur-Soulzon	42	C4
Rosans	38	C4
Roscoff	14	B3
Rosporden	14	B1
Rostassac	35	F2
Rostrenen	14	C2
Rothéneuf	15	E3
Rotterdam	5	D3
Roubaix	11	F3
Rouen	17	F4
Rouffach	21	E2
Rouge	23	D4
Rougemont	21	D1
Rougemont	27	E4
Rouillac	29	D2
Roujan	43	D3
Roulers (Roeselare)	4	B1
Roussillon	38	B3
Rouvres-en-Xaintois	20	C2
Royan	28	B2
Royat	31	D2
Roybon	32	B2
Roye	11	E1
Royère	30	B2
Rozay-en-Brie	18	C3
Rozoy	12	B3
Rue	11	D3
Ruelle	29	D2
Ruffec	29	D2
Ruffieux	32	C3
Rugles	17	E2
Rumigny	12	C3
Rumilly	32	C3
Rupt	21	D2
Ruurlo	6	B3

S

Saales	21	E2
Sables-d'Or	15	D3
Sablé-sur-Sarthe	23	F4
Sabres	34	C1
Saeul	9	D2
Sagone	44	B2
Saillagouse	42	B1
Saillans	32	B1
Sains	12	B3
Sainte Anne-d'Auray	22	A4
Sainte Anne-la-Palud	14	A2
Sainte Croix-Volvestre	41	F2
Sainte Enimie	37	D2
Sainte Foy-la-Grande	35	D3
Sainte Gauburge-Sainte Colombe	17	E2
Sainte Hélène	34	C3
Sainte Hermine	28	B4

Sainte Marie-aux-Mines	21	E2
Sainte Marie-de-Campan	41	D2
Sainte Maries-de-la-Mer	43	F3
Sainte Maure-de-Touraine	24	A2
Sainte Maxime	39	E1
Sainte Menehould	13	D2
Sainte Mère-Église	16	B4
Saintes	28	C2
Sainte Sévère	30	B3
Sainte Suzanne	23	F4

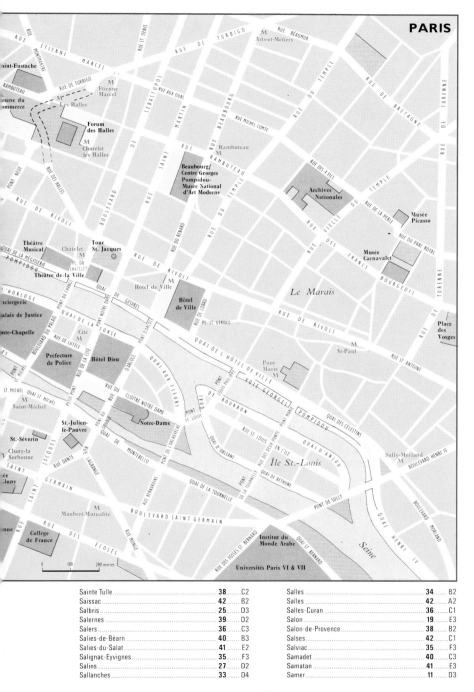

Samoëns	33	D4
Sanary	38	C1
Sancergues	25	E2
Sancerre	25	E3
Sancoins	25	E2
Sanguinet	34	B2
Santa Maria-Siche	44	B2
Santa Severa	44	C4
Sappemeer	3	E3
Saramon	41	E3
Sarlat-la-Canéda	35	F3
Sarralbe	21	D4
Sarrebourg	21	D3
Sarreguemines	21	D4
Sarre-Union	21	D4
Sarron	40	C3
Sartène	44	B1
Sartilly	16	B2
Sarzeau	22	B3
Sassenage	32	C2
Sassenheim	5	D4
Saucats	34	C3
Saugues	37	D3
Saujon	28	C2
Saulieu	26	B3
Sault	38	C3
Saulx	20	C1
Saulxures	21	D2
Saumur	23	F2
Sauve	43	E4
Sauveterre-de-Béarn	40	B3
Sauveterre-de-Guyenne	35	D3
Sauxillanges	31	D1
Sauzé-Vaussais	29	D3
Sauzon	22	A3
Savenay	22	C3
Saverdun	42	A2
Saverne	21	E3
Savignac-les-Eglises	35	E4
Savigny-sur-Braye	24	B4
Savines-le-Lac	39	D4
Scaër	14	B1
Schagen	2	C2
Scheveningen	4	C4
Schiermonnikoog	3	D3
Schilde	5	D2
Schirmeck	21	E3
Schoondijke	4	B2
Schoonebeek	3	E1
Schoonhoven	5	D3
Schoonoord	3	E2
Seclin	11	F3
Secondigny	28	C4
Sedan	13	D3
Séderon	38	C3
Sées	17	D2
Segonzac	29	D2
Segré	23	E3
Seiches	23	E3
Seilhac	36	A4
Sélestat	21	E2
Selles	24	C3
Sellières	27	D2
Selongey	26	C4
Seltz	21	F4
Semur-en-Auxois	26	B4
Sénas	38	B2
Senlis	18	C4
Sennecey-le-Grand	26	C2
Senonches	17	E2
Senones	21	D3
Sens	19	D2

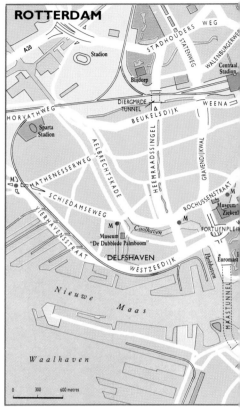

Sept-Saulx	12	C2
Seraing	9	D4
Sérent	22	B4
Sermaize-les-Bains	20	A3
Serres	38	C4
Serrières	32	A2
Sète	43	E3
Seurre	26	C3
Sévérac-le-Château	37	D2
Sevrier	33	D3
Seyches	35	D2
Seyne	39	D4
Seyssel	32	C4
Sézanne	19	D3
's Heerenberg	6	B3
Sierck	13	F2
Sierentz	21	E1
Sigean	42	C2
Signy-l'Abbaye	12	C3
Sillé-le-Guillaume	17	D1
Siorac-en-Périgord	35	F3
Sisteron	38	C3
Sittard	5	F1
Six-Fours	38	C1
Sizun	14	B2
Sliedrecht	5	D3
Sloten	3	D2

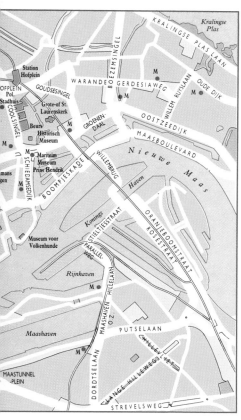

Soustons	40	B3
Souvigny	31	D3
Spa	9	D3
Spakenburg	5	E4
Spijkenisse	4	C3
Spincourt	13	E2
St Abbs	34	C4
St Affrique	42	C4
St Agnant	28	B2
St Agrève	37	F3
St Aignan	24	C3
St Aignan	23	D4
St Aignan	33	G4
St Alban	37	D3
St Amand-en-Puisaye	25	E3
St Amand-les-Eaux	12	A4
St Amand Longpré	24	B4
St Amans	37	D2
St Amant-Roche-Savine	31	D1
St Ambroix	37	E2
St Amé	21	D2
St Amour	26	C1
St André	17	F2
St André-du-Cubzac	34	C3
St André-les-Alpes	39	D3
St Annaparochie	3	D3
St Anthème	31	E1
St Antonin-Noble-Val	36	A1
St Armand-Montrond	25	D2
St Aubin-d'Aubigné	16	A1
St Aubin-du-Cormier	16	B1
St Aubin-sur-Mer	16	C3
St Aulaye	35	D4
St Avold	13	F2
St Aygulf	39	E2
St Bard Maison Rouge	30	C2
St Béat	41	E2
St Beauzély	36	C1
St Benin	25	F2
St Benoît	30	A3
St Benoit-sur-Loire	25	D4
St Bertrand-de-Comminges	41	E2
St Blin	20	B2
St Bonnet	33	D1
St Bonnet de Joux	31	F3
St Bonnet-le-Chateau	31	E1
St Brévin	22	C2
St Brice-en-Coglès	16	B2
St Brieuc	15	D2
St Calais	24	B4
St Cast	15	E3
St Céré	36	B3
St Cernin	36	B3
St Chamas	38	B2
St Chamond	31	F1
St Chély-d'Apcher	37	D3
St Chely-d'Aubrac	36	C2
St Chinian	42	C3
St Ciers	34	C4
St Clar	41	E4
St Claud	29	E2
St Claude	27	D1
St Cyprien	35	F3
St Cyprien-Plage	43	D1
St Denis	18	B3
St Denis d'Oléron	28	B3
St Denis d'Orques	23	F4
St Didier-en-Velay	37	F4
St Dié	21	D2
St Dizier	20	A3
St Donat-sur-l'Herbasse	32	B2
St Emilion	35	D3

Sluis	4	B2
Sluis	4	C3
Smilde	3	E2
Sneek	3	D2
Soest	5	E4
Soestdijk	5	E4
Soignies	8	B4
Soissons	12	A2
Solenzara	44	C2
Solliès-Pont	39	D1
Sombernon	26	B3
Sommesous	19	E3
Sommières	43	E3
Sore	34	C2
Sospel	39	F3
Sotta	44	B1
Souesmes	25	D3
Soufflenheim	21	F4
Souillac	36	A3
Souilly	13	D1
Soulac	28	B1
Soultz	21	E1
Soultz	21	F4
Soumoulou	41	D2
Souppes	18	C2
Sourdeval	16	B2
Sousceyrac	36	B3

St Etienne	31	F1
St Etienne	38	C3
St Etienne-de-Baigorry	40	B2
St Etienne-de-St-Geoirs	32	B2
St Etienne-de-Tinée	39	E3
St Fargeau	25	E3
St Firmin	32	C1
St Florent	23	D3
St Florent	25	D2
St Florent	44	C3
St Florentin	19	D1
St Flour	37	D3
St Fulgent	23	D2
St Galmier	31	F1
St Gaudens	41	E2
St Gaultier	24	C1
St Geniez-d'Olt	36	C2
St Genis-de-Saintonge	28	C1
St Genix	32	C3
St Georges	23	E3
St Georges-de-Didonne	28	B2
St Geours-de-Maremne	40	B3
St Germain	18	B3
St Germain	30	A2
St Germain-de-Joux	32	C4
St Germain-des-Vaux	16	A4
St Germain-du-Bois	26	C2
St Germain-du-Plain	26	C2
St Germain-Laval	31	E2
St Germain-Lembron	31	D1
St Germain-l'Herm	31	D1
St Germain-Plage	16	A3
St Gervais	33	D3
St Gervais	43	D3
St Gervais-d'Auvergne	30	C2
St Géry	36	A2
St Gildas-des-Bois	22	C3
St Gilles	43	F3
St Gilles-Croix-de-Vie	22	C1
St Giron-Plage	40	B4
St Girons	41	F2
St Gorgan-Main	27	E3
St Guénolé	14	A1
St Hilaire-de-Villefranche	28	C2
St Hilaire-du-Harcouët	16	B2
St Hippolyte	27	F3
St Hippolyte-du-Fort	43	E4
St Honoré	26	A2
St Hubert	9	D2
St Jacut	15	E2
St James	16	B2
St Jean-Brévelay	22	B4
St Jean-Cap-Ferrat	39	F2
St Jean-d'Angély	28	C2
St Jean-de-Bournay	32	B3
St Jean-de-Losne	26	C3
St Jean-de-Luz	40	A3
St Jean-de-Maurienne	33	D2
St Jean-de-Monts	22	C2
St Jean du Bruel	37	D1
St Jean du Gard	37	E1
St Jean-le-Thomas	16	B2
St Jean-Pied-de-Port	40	B2
St Jeoire	33	D4
St Jorioz	33	D3
St Jouan-de-l'Isle	15	E2
St Julien-Chapteuil	37	E3
St Julien-de-Vouvantes	23	D3
St Julien-en-Beauchêne	38	C4
St Julien-en-Genevois	32	C4
St Julien-l'Ars	29	E4
St Junien	29	E2

St Just-en-Chaussée	11	E1
St Just-en-Chevalet	31	E2
St Justin	41	D4
St Lary-Soulan	41	D1
St Laurent	16	C4
St Laurent	29	F2
St Laurent-en-Grandvaux	27	D2
St Laurent-et-Benon	34	C4
St Leger	26	A2
St Léonard-de-Noblat	30	A2
St Lô	16	B3
St Louis	21	E1
St Loup-sur-Semouse	20	C1
St Lunaire	15	E3
St Lys	41	F3
St Macaire	35	D2
St Maclou	17	E3

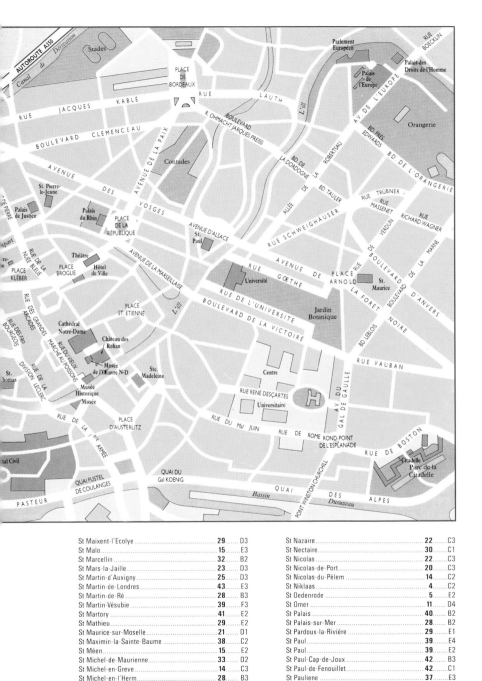

St Maixent-l'Ecolye	29	D3
St Malo	15	E3
St Marcellin	32	B2
St Mars-la-Jaille	23	D3
St Martin-d'Auxigny	25	D3
St Martin-de-Londres	43	E3
St Martin-de-Ré	28	B3
St Martin-Vésubie	39	F3
St Martory	41	E2
St Mathieu	29	E2
St Maurice-sur-Moselle	21	D1
St Maximin-la-Sainte-Baume	38	C2
St Méen	15	E2
St Michel-de-Maurienne	33	D2
St Michel-en-Greve	14	C3
St Michel-en-l'Herm	28	B3
St Mihiel	20	B4

St Nazaire	22	C3
St Nectaire	30	C1
St Nicolas	22	C3
St Nicolas-de-Port	20	C3
St Nicolas-du-Pélem	14	C2
St Niklaas	4	C2
St Oedenrode	5	E2
St Omer	11	D4
St Palais	40	B2
St Palais-sur-Mer	28	B2
St Pardoux-la-Rivière	29	E1
St Paul	39	E4
St Paul	39	E2
St Paul-Cap-de-Joux	42	B3
St Paul-de-Fenouillet	42	C1
St Pauliene	37	E3
St Pé	41	D2

St Péray .... **32** A1
St Père-en-Retz .... **22** C2
St Philbert .... **22** C2
St Pierre-d'Albigny .... **33** D3
St Pierre-de-Chartreuse .... **32** C2
St Pierre-de-Chignac .... **35** E3
St Pierre-d'Oléron .... **28** B2
St Pierre-Église .... **16** B4
St Pierre-le-Moûtier .... **25** E2
St Pierre-Quiberon .... **22** A3
St Pierre-sur-Dives .... **17** D3
St Pois .... **16** B2
St Pol-de-Léon .... **14** B3
St Pol-sur-Ternoise .... **11** E3
St Pons .... **42** C3
St Porchaire .... **28** C2
St Pourcain .... **31** D3
St Privat .... **36** B3
St Quay-Portrieux .... **15** D3
St Quentin .... **12** A3
St Rambert-d'Albon .... **32** A2
St Rambert-en-Bugey ...... **32** B3
St Raphael .... **39** E2
St Rémy-de-Provence .... **38** B2
St Renan .... **14** A2
St Riquier .... **11** D2
St Rome-de-Tarn .... **36** C1
St Saëns .... **10** C1
St Satur .... **25** E3
St Saulge .... **25** F2
St Sauvant .... **29** D3
St Sauveur-en-Puisaye ..... **25** F4
St Sauveur-le-Vicomte ..... **16** B4
St Sauveur-sur-Tiné .... **39** E3
St Savin .... **29** E4
St Savin .... **34** C4
St Seine-l'Abbaye .... **26** B3
St Sernin-sur-Rance .... **42** C4
St Sever .... **16** B2
St Sever .... **40** C3
St Symphorien .... **34** C2
St Symphorien-de Lay ..... **31** E2
St Symphorien-d'Ozon .... **32** B3
St Symphorien-sur-Coise .. **31** F2
St Thiébault .... **20** B2
St Trivier-de-Courtes .... **26** C1
St Tropez .... **39** D1
St Truiden .... **5** E1
St Vaast-la-Hougue .... **16** B4
St Valery-en-Caux .... **10** B2
St Valery-sur-Somme .... **11** D2
St Vallier-de-Thiey .... **39** E2
St Vallier-sur-Rhône .... **32** A2
St Vaury .... **30** B3
St Véran .... **33** E1
St Vincent-de-Tyrosse ..... **40** B3
St Vith .... **9** E3
St Vivien-de-Médoc .... **28** B1
St Yrieix-la-Perche .... **29** F1
Stadskanaal .... **3** F2
Stainville .... **20** B3
Stavelot .... **9** D3
Stavenisse .... **4** C3
Staveren .... **2** C2
Steenbergen .... **4** C3
Steenvoorde .... **11** E4
Steenwijk .... **3** D2
Stellendam .... **4** C3
Stenay .... **13** D2
Stiens .... **3** D3
Strasbourg .... **21** E3
Suippes .... **12** C2

Sully .... **25** D4
Surgères .... **28** C3
Survilliers .... **18** C4
Swalmen .... **5** F2

T

Tain-l'Hermitage .... **32** A2
Tallard .... **39** D4
Talloires .... **33** D3
Talmont .... **28** C1
Talmont-St-Hilaire .... **28** A3
Tancarville .... **17** E4
Taninges .... **33** D4
Tarare .... **31** F2
Tarascon .... **38** A2
Tarascon-sur-Ariège .... **42** A1
Tarbes .... **41** D2
Tardets-Sorholus .... **40** B2
Tarnos .... **40** A3
Tartas .... **40** B4
Tauves .... **30** C1
Tavaux .... **26** C3
Tavernes .... **39** D2
Tegelen .... **5** F2
Temse .... **4** C2
Tence .... **37** F3
Tende .... **39** F3
Ter Apel .... **3** F2
Terneuzen .... **4** C2
Terrasson-la-Villedieu ..... **35** F3
Tervuren .... **5** D1
Tessy .... **16** B3
Thann .... **21** E1
Thénezay .... **23** F1
Thenon .... **35** F3
Théoule .... **39** E2
Thérouanne .... **11** D3
Theux .... **9** D3
Thiaucourt .... **13** E1
Thiberville .... **17** E3
Thiéblemont-Farémont ..... **19** F3
Thiers .... **31** D2
Thionville .... **13** E2
Thivars .... **17** F1
Thiviers .... **29** E1
Thizy .... **31** F2
Thoissey .... **32** A4
Thonon .... **27** E1
Thouarce .... **23** E2
Thouars .... **23** F2
Thueyts .... **37** E2
Thuir .... **42** C1
Thury-Harcourt .... **16** C3
Tiel .... **5** E3
Tielt .... **4** B1
Tienen .... **5** D1
Tierce .... **23** E3
Tignes .... **33** E3
Tilburg .... **5** D2
Til-Châtel .... **26** C4
Tinchebray .... **16** C2
Tongeren (Tongres) .... **5** E1
Tongres (Tongeren) .... **5** E1
Tonnay-Boutonne .... **28** C2
Tonnay-Charente .... **28** C2
Tonneins .... **35** D2
Tonnerre .... **19** E1
Torhout .... **4** A2

Torigni	16	B3
Tôtes	10	C1
Toucy	25	F4
Toul	20	C3
Toulon	38	C1
Toulon-sur-Arroux	26	A2
Toulouse	42	A3
Tourcoing	11	F3
Tournai (Doornik)	8	A4
Tournan	18	C3
Tournay	41	D2
Tournon	32	A2
Tournon-d'Agenais	35	F2
Tournon-St-Martin	24	B2
Tournus	26	C2
Tours	24	B3
Toury	18	B2
Trébeurden	14	C3
Tréboul	14	A2
Trégastel	14	C3
Tréguier	14	C3
Treignac	30	B1
Trets	38	C2
Trévoux	32	A3
Triaize	28	B3
Triaucourt	13	D1
Trie	41	D2
Troarn	17	D3
Trois-Ponts	9	D3
Trouville	17	D3
Troyes	19	E2
Truchtersheim	21	E3
Trun	17	D2
Tuchan	42	C2
Tuffe	17	E1
Tulle	36	A4
Tullins	32	C2
Turckheim	21	E2
Turnhout	5	D2
Tzummarum	3	D3

U

Uckange	13	E2
Uden	5	E3
Ugine	33	D3
Uithoorn	5	D4
Uithuizen	3	E3
Urdos	40	C1
Urk	3	D2
Ury	18	C2
Ussel	30	B1
Ustaritz	40	A3
Utrecht	5	E4
Uzel	15	D2
Uzerche	30	A1
Uzès	37	F1

V

Vaas	24	A4
Vaassen	6	A4
Vaiges	23	E4
Vailly	12	A2
Vailly	25	E3
Vaison-la-Romaine	38	B3

Valberg	39	E3
Valbonnais	32	C1
Val-Claret	33	E2
Valdahon	27	E3
Val d'Esquières	39	E1
Val d'Isère	33	E3
Valençay	24	C2
Valence	32	B1
Valence	35	E1
Valence	41	E4
Valence d'Albigeois	36	B1
Valenciennes	12	A4
Valensole	39	D3
Valkenburg	5	F1
Valkenswaard	5	E2
Valleraugue	37	E1
Vallet	23	D2
Valloire	33	D2
Vallon en Sully	30	C3
Vallon-Pont-d'Arc	37	F2
Vallorcine	33	E4
Vallouise	33	D1
Valmorel	33	D2
Valognes	16	B4
Valras-Plage	43	D2
Valréas	38	B4
Vals-les-Bains	37	F2
Val-Suzon	26	C3
Vannes	22	B3
Varades	23	D3
Varces	32	C2
Varengeville	10	C2
Varennes-en-Argonne	13	D2
Varennes-sur-Allier	31	D3
Varilhes	42	A2
Vars	39	E4
Varsseveld	6	B3
Varzy	25	F3
Vassy	16	C2
Vatan	24	C2
Vaucouleurs	20	B3
Vauvert	43	F3
Vauville	16	A4
Vauvillers	20	C2
Vayrac	36	A3
Veendam	3	E3
Veenendaal	5	E3
Veere	4	B3
Veghel	5	E3
Veldhoven	5	E2
Velp	6	A3
Venaco	44	B3
Vence	39	E2
Vendargues	43	E3
Vendeuvre	19	E2
Vendôme	24	B4
Venlo	5	F2
Venray	5	F2
Verberie	18	C4
Verdun	13	D2
Verfeil	42	A3
Vergt	35	E3
Vermenton	26	A4
Vernet	42	A3
Vernet-les-Bains	42	B1
Verneuil	17	E2
Vernon	18	A4
Verny	13	F1
Versailles	18	B3
Verteillac	35	E4
Vertus	19	E3
Verviers	9	D4

Vervins	12	B3
Verzy	12	B2
Vesoul	27	E4
Veules-les-Roses	10	B2
Veulettes-sur-Mer	10	B2
Veurne (Furnès)	4	A2
Veynes	38	C4
Veyrier	33	D3
Vézelay	26	A4
Vézelise	20	C3
Vézénobres	37	E1
Viais	23	D2
Vianden	9	E2
Vianen	5	D3
Vianne	35	D2
Vias	43	D2
Vibraye	24	B4
Vic	31	D2
Vicdessos	42	A1
Vic-en-Bigorre	41	D3
Vic-Fezensac	41	D3
Vichy	31	D3
Vico	44	B2
Vic-sur-Aisne	18	C4
Vic-sur-Cère	36	C3
Vidauban	39	D2
Vielsalm	9	D3
Vienne	32	B3
Vierzon	25	D3
Vieux-Boucau	40	B3
Vif	32	C2
Vigneulles	13	E1
Vignory	20	A2
Vihiers	23	E2
Villaines-la-Juhel	16	C1
Villandraut	34	C2
Villandry	24	A2
Villard-de-lans	32	C2
Villars	27	E3
Villars	39	E3
Villars-les-Dombes	32	B4
Villé	21	E3
Villebois Lavalette	29	D1
Villedieu-les-Poêles	16	B3
Ville-en-Tardenois	12	B2
Villefagnan	29	D2
Villefort	37	E2
Villefranche	39	F2
Villefranche-d'Albigeois	42	B4
Villefranche-de-Lauragais	42	A3
Villefranche-de-Lonchat	35	D3
Villefranche-de-Rouergue	36	B2
Villefranche-du-Périgord	35	F2
Villefranche-sur-Cher	24	C3
Villefranche-sur-Saone	32	A4
Villemur	42	A4
Villenauxe-la-Grande	19	D2
Villeneuve	36	B2
Villeneuve	38	A3
Villeneuve-de-Berg	37	F2
Villeneuve-de-Marsan	40	C4
Villeneuve-l'Archevêque	19	D2
Villeneuve-Loubet	39	E2
Villeneuve-sur-Allier	25	F1
Villeneuve-sur-Lot	35	E2
Villeneuve-sur-Yonne	19	D1
Villeréal	35	E2
Villers	17	D3
Villers Bocage	16	C3
Villers-Bretonneux	11	E2
Villers-Cotterêts	18	C4
Villersexel	27	E4
Villers-St.Georges	19	D3
Villerville	17	D4
Vimoutiers	17	D4
Vinay	32	B2
Vinca	42	C1
Vinon-sur-Verdon	38	C2
Vire	16	C2
Virieu	32	C3
Virieu-le-Grand	32	C3
Virton	9	D1
Visé	9	D4
Vitré	16	B1
Vitry-le-François	19	F3
Vitteaux	26	B3
Vittel	20	C2
Vivario	44	B2
Viviers	38	A4
Vivonne	29	D3
Vizille	32	C2
Vizzavona	44	B2
Vlaardingen	4	C3
Vlagtweede	3	F2
Vlissingen	4	B2
Void	20	B3
Voiron	32	C2
Voise	18	A2
Voix	38	C3
Volendam	2	C1
Voorschoten	5	D4
Voorst	6	B4
Voreppe	32	C2
Vorey	37	E4
Vouillé	29	D4
Vouvray	24	B4
Vouziers	12	C2
Voves	18	A2
Vresse	8	C2
Vron	11	D3
Vroomshoop	3	E1
Vught	5	E3

W

Waalwijk	5	D3
Wageningen	5	E3
Wangenbourg	21	E3
Waregem	4	B1
Waremme	8	C4
Warnsveld	6	B4
Wasselone	21	E3
Wassenaar	4	C4
Wasserbillig	9	E3
Wassy	20	A3
Waterloo	8	B4
Waulsort	8	C3
Wavre	8	C4
Weert	5	E2
Well	5	F2
Wellin	8	C3
Wemperhaardt	9	E3
Wépion	8	C3
Werbomont	9	D3
Westende-Bad	4	A2
Westerlo	5	D1
Westkapelle	4	B2
West-Terchelling	2	C3
Wetteren	4	C1
Wierden	6	B4
Wijhe	6	B4

Willebroek

Willebroek .... **4** C1
Willemstad .... **5** D3
Wiltz .... **9** D2
Wimereux .... **11** D4
Winschoten .... **3** F3
Winsum .... **3** E3
Winterswijk .... **6** B3
Wissant .... **11** D4
Wissembourg .... **21** F4
Woerden .... **5** D4
Wœrth .... **21** E4
Wolvega .... **3** D2
Workum .... **2** C2
Wormerveer .... **2** B1
Wormhout .... **11** E4
Wuustwezel .... **5** D2

X

Xertigny .... **21** D2
Xhoffraix .... **9** E3

Y

Yenne .... **32** C3
Yerville .... **10** B1
Yport .... **10** B1
Ypres (Ieper) .... **4** A1
Yssingeaux .... **37** E3
Yvetot .... **10** B1
Yvoir .... **8** C3
Yvoire .... **27** E1

Z

Zaandam .... **2** B1
Zaltbommel .... **5** E3
Zandvoort .... **2** B1
Zeebrugge .... **4** B2
Zeist .... **5** E4
Zelzate .... **4** C2
Zevenaar .... **6** A3
Zevenergen .... **5** D3
Zicavo .... **44** B2
Zierikzee .... **4** C3
Zijpe .... **4** C3
Zoetermeer .... **5** D4
Zolder .... **5** E1
Zonza .... **44** B1
Zoutkamp .... **3** E3
Zuidhorn .... **3** E3
Zuidlaren .... **3** E2
Zundert .... **5** D2
Zutphen .... **6** B4
Zwijndrecht .... **5** D3
Zwolle .... **3** D1

Distance chart
(kilometres)

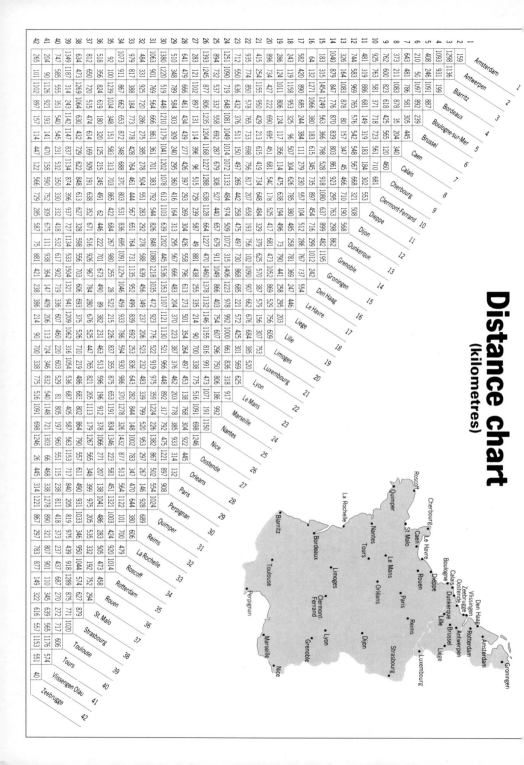